TONY'S VIRUS

Steven E. Greer, MD

"Today, we are very honored to have Dr. Steven Greer, who is a really accomplished doctor and also a Wall Street expert. Having been in a number of other fields, including investment banking, he brings a broad perspective to this."

Rudy Giuliani
Common Sense podcast
Former U.S. Attorney, former Mayor of New York City, and current lawyer for President Trump

For all Americans living in poverty, fear, and poor health as a result of the far-left anarchists trying to topple the United States of America by any means possible, including the exploitation of a pandemic.

October 22, 2020

Table of Contents

Foreword: How the Hell did this Happen?

It was the Memorial Day holiday, May 25th, 2020, right as much of Florida had begun lifting the Wuhan virus pandemic lockdown orders. I was driving South on Highway 1 in Port Saint Lucie and saw numerous "for rent" signs on establishments that had gone out of business. However, I also saw that the "big-box" stores, such as Walmart, were still in business and doing well.

Few in the media were talking about this: globalist companies like Amazon and Walmart were thriving as small American businesses failed. How did this happen?

Walmart is basically a subsidiary of the country of China. Everything they sell is from China. Yet China created the Wuhan virus pandemic, as will be explained.[1] Chinese companies made money from Americans via Walmart and small American shops were run out of business by arbitrary government decrees? What?

Amazon is another seller of Chinese counterfeit goods and also profited greatly from the pandemic lockdowns. Owner Jeff Bezos can survive a lifetime of economic depression given his personal wealth. He is a staunch opponent of President Trump and might not think twice about destroying the U.S. economy if it meant hurting Trump. All the while, Bezos gained billions in net worth from the pandemic as distressed Americans under house-arrest were forced to use Amazon?

So, these big-box globalist companies with Democrat CEO's are benefitting from virus windfalls as small American companies were put out of business. Say what?

---

[11] The Wuhan virus is also known as SARS-CoV-2, the coronavirus, or the propaganda term COVID-19 created by the World Health Organization to obfuscate the origin of the pandemic, as will be explained later.

One can't even blame Democrat governors because all of this I observed was happening in Florida, a red state with a Republican governor. Huh?

I then reached my destination, which was a coffee shop at a marina in Stuart, Florida. I was sitting next to three college girls. I asked them whether they were still paying tuition despite the fact that their schools had shut down. They were.

That was another big story that I had not heard discussed in the media. College has always been a scam. Now it is even worse. The colleges are taking huge amounts of money away from these kids, putting them into a lifetime of debt, and not even providing them with an education at all now? Moreover, there is no need to shut down colleges. We now know the biological reason for the Wuhan virus attacking elderly and not the young. Younger people do not have the ACE-2 receptors on the cells in their nose that the virus uses.[2] The percentage of college students who would get sick from this virus is no more than any other illness like the regular flu.

The education in most of these liberal arts schools has long been speculative and mostly useless for the real world. Now, they are not even bothering to give an education. Why don't they just hand out diplomas in exchange for money? That's pretty much what they have been doing all along.

The way that the globalist elite establishment, from colleges to big-box store CEOs, has profited from this pandemic is mind-blowing. How the hell did this happen?

Not only did the rich get richer and the middle-class get hammered by the scamdemic, but the entire healthcare system has all but shut down for more than six-months. Unknown numbers of people will die soon from cancers

---

[2] Bunyavanich S, et al "Nasal Gene Expression of Angiotensin-Converting Enzyme 2 in Children and Adults" JAMA. Published online May 20, 2020.

that could have been diagnosed earlier. They have suffered with treatable illnesses, such as orthopedic pain. Mental illness has been fueled by the unemployment and house-arrest orders leading to unknown numbers of suicides and drug overdoses. Weaknesses in our hospital system were exposed as thousands of people needlessly died due to negligent care. Who will be pay for these deaths?

I have been asked these questions many times since I began to do media interviews in March of 2020. A common thread to many of my talks about the pandemic has been Anthony Fauci, MD, the Director of the NIH's National Institute of Allergy and Infectious Diseases (NIAID), or simply Tony as President Trump calls him. He was involved from the nidus of it all, in his laboratories that create dangerous new strains of viruses, such as the as the SARS-CoV-2 or Wuhan virus, on up to the policy level and decisions that led to the closure of much of the global economy.

In this book, I aim to consolidate my hours of discussion and numerous essays on the Great Scamdemic. Rather than make this a boring scientific book, I try to humanize it and tell the story of Tony Fauci and his virus.

Chapter 1: In the Beginning

> "In the beginning God created the heavens and the earth.
>
> And God said, "Let there be light," and, "Let the water teem with living creatures."
>
> Then God said, "Let us make mankind in our image, in our likeness, so that they may rule over the fish in the sea and the birds in the sky, over the livestock and all the wild animals, and over all the creatures that move along the ground."
>
> Then Tony Fauci said, "Let us improve upon God's work and create viruses in our NIH labs"" - The New Book of Genesis

Where did the "COVID-19" or "Wuhan virus" originate? Was it a normal mutation in nature or did humans create it in a bioweapons lab?

First, let's settle on a proper name. The name for the virus that caused the Great Scamdemic of 2020 is the SARS-CoV-2, which is short for Severe Acute Respiratory Syndrome-coronavirus-2. The number 2 indicates that it is the second "SARS" virus that has caused an outbreak. The first one was in 2002.

COVID-19, which stands for Coronavirus Disease 2019, is a nonscientific name dreamed up the World Health

Organization (W.H.O.).[3] The Director-General of the W.H.O., Tedros Adhanom Ghebreyesus, explained on February 11, 2020,

> "Having a name matters to prevent the use of other names that can be inaccurate or stigmatizing."[4] He also tweeted on February 11, 2020, "Under agreed guidelines between WHO, the @OIEAnimalHealth & @FAO, we had to find a name that did not refer to a geographical location, an animal, an individual or group of people, and which is also pronounceable and related to the disease"-@DrTedros #COVID19"

To what was he alluding? What group of people was he protecting from being stigmatized?

The W.H.O. has long been in cahoots with the Chinese Communist Party, which is why the Trump administration cut funding.[5] The world knew that the SARS-CoV-2 outbreak started in Wuhan, China. Viruses causing pandemics are often given nicknames based on the locations of origin. Therefore, in a feckless and transparent move, the W.H.O. engaged in classic George Orwell doublespeak to help the Chinese in their own propaganda campaign aimed at shedding blame.

Nevertheless, the term Wuhan virus caught on thanks to its use by President Trump. This author was one

---

[3] Yuen K, et al. "SARS-CoV-2 and COVID-19: The most important research questions" Cell Biosci. V 10, 2020.

[4] WHO Director-General's remarks at the media briefing on 2019-nCoV. February 11, 2020

[5] "Coronavirus: Trump accuses WHO of being a puppet of China". May 19, 2020.

of the first to popularize it on New York radio stations[6] and books[7]. Just like the Spanish Flu of 1918, the Wuhan virus is a name that will go down in infamy. [8]

The term COVID-19 should really not be used at all due to its duplicitous origins of propaganda. However, if one does choose to use it, the term refers only to the constellation of symptoms of the illness and not the actual virus, like AIDS is to the HIV virus or shingles is to the herpes virus. It is completely wrong to call it the "COVID virus".

Back to the question of origin, the SARS-CoV-2 virus first started to spread in Wuhan, China. There is no doubt about that, as will be detailed below. For a while, the Chinese government was trying to claim that it started in Italy or the United States.[9]

But how? Was the Wuhan virus created by animal-to-human spread in "wet markets" selling grotesque animals like bats for human consumption? Or, did the nearby American-NIH-funded virology lab in Wuhan let it escape? The intelligence community believes it is the latter.

When congressional intelligence committees were first briefed by Tony Fauci, the CIA, and other sources on the threat of the Wuhan virus in late January and early February of 2020, they were clearly given a scary story of a manmade virus that escaped from the Wuhan lab. It caused

---

[6] Radio appearances by Steven E. Greer: https://greerjournal.com/radio-appearances-by-steven-e-greer-md/

[7] Greer SE. "Rules to Stop Radicals" Amazon and Barnes & Noble presses. 2019, 2020

[8] Actually, the influenza virus of 1918 would have been more accurately called the "Western Front" virus because American soldiers in trench warfare of WW1 carried it back to a Kansas military base.

[9] They actually have an argument that it did start in the United States, at least genetically and funding-wise, as will be discussed later.

some members of congress to allegedly violate the law and sell personal stock investments before the information became public.

Forbes reported,

"Four U.S. senators sold stock after receiving sensitive briefings in late January about the emerging threat of the coronavirus...

Senator Richard Burr, a Republican from North Carolina, and Kelly Loeffler, a Republican from Georgia, both completed their sales at a time when the Trump administration and GOP leaders were downplaying the potential damage the virus might cause in the U.S. and before drastic stock-market plunges set off by the pandemic...Two other members of the Intelligence Committee, Senator Dianne Feinstein... and Senator James Inhofe...also sold stock after the briefings...

Loeffler did not make any sales from Jan. 6 until Jan. 24 -- the day the health committee she sits on held a briefing that included presentations from top level U.S. public-health officials including Dr. Anthony Fauci. She and her husband began selling 27 stocks on Jan. 24, according to her financial disclosure form...worth millions of dollars."[10]

That was clearly panic selling. Those congresspersons were not told by Tony Fauci that this was

[10] Kocieniewski D. "4 U.S. senators sold stock after getting coronavirus threat briefings in January" Forbes. March 20, 2020

a normal variant of a virus found in nature. Senator Tom Cotton, a member of the Senate Select Committee on Intelligence, was briefed by Fauci and began telling the press that there was strong evidence to support the theory that the virus leaked from a lab.

In a Wall Street Journal Op-Ed, Cotton wrote,

"The U.S. government is investigating whether the Covid-19 virus came from a government laboratory in Wuhan, China. Beijing has claimed that the virus originated in a Wuhan "wet market," where wild animals were sold. But evidence to counter this theory emerged in January. Chinese researchers reported in the Lancet Jan. 24 that the first known cases had no contact with the market, and Chinese state media acknowledged the finding. There's no evidence the market sold bats or pangolins, the animals from which the virus is thought to have jumped to humans. And the bat species that carries it isn't found within 100 miles of Wuhan.

Wuhan has two labs where we know bats and humans interacted. One is the Wuhan Institute of Virology, eight miles from the wet market; the other is the Wuhan Center for Disease Control and Prevention, barely 300 yards from the market.

Both labs collect live animals to study viruses. Their researchers travel to caves across China to capture bats for this purpose. Chinese state media released a minidocumentary in mid-December following a team of Wuhan CDC researchers collecting viruses from bats in caves. The researchers fretted openly about the risk of infection.

These risks were not limited to the field. The Washington Post reported last week that in 2018 U.S. diplomats in China warned of "a serious shortage of appropriately trained technicians and investigators needed to safely operate" the Institute of Virology. The Wuhan CDC operates at even lower biosafety standards.

While the Chinese government denies the possibility of a lab leak, its actions tell a different story. The Chinese military posted its top epidemiologist to the Institute of Virology in January. In February Chairman Xi Jinping urged swift implementation of new biosafety rules to govern pathogens in laboratory settings. Academic papers about the virus's origins are now subject to prior restraint by the government.

In early January, enforcers threatened doctors who warned their colleagues about the virus. Among them was Li Wenliang, who died of Covid-19 in February. Laboratories working to sequence the virus's genetic code were ordered to destroy their samples. The laboratory that first published the virus's genome was shut down, Hong Kong's South China Morning Post reported in February.

This evidence is circumstantial, to be sure, but it all points toward the Wuhan labs. Thanks to the Chinese coverup, we may never have direct, conclusive evidence-intelligence rarely works that way-but Americans justifiably can use common sense to follow the inherent logic of events to their likely conclusion."[11]

---

[11] Cotton T. "Cotton Op-Ed in the Wall Street Journal 'Coronavirus and the Laboratories in Wuhan'" Website of Senator Tom Cotton https://www.cotton.senate.gov April 21, 2020

The really dangerous next question to ask is whether the Wuhan virus was simply being curated and stored in the Wuhan labs or was actually genetically engineered? Creating deadly viruses would be considered a bioweapons program, or weapons of mass destruction (WMD): The reason that the U.S. started the wars with Iraq and Afghanistan.[12] The Chinese and American governments would certainly try to cover that up. Have they?

First, let's address the controversy of the low-budget documentary called *Plandemic* that focused on the tumultuous career of PhD virologist Judy Mikovits. The claims made in the film stirred up the veritable hornets' nest and generated obvious partisan attacks designed to discredit her. Therefore, we know that she had something truthful to say and was a threat to Tony Fauci, his NIH group, and the military.

Mikovits claims that she worked at the Army Biolabs at Fort Detrick in Maryland near the NIH that funds the scientific labs inside. That is true and Tony Fauci, *et al* do not deny that. She also claims that the lab, and others like it, use genetic engineering to create manmade strains of viruses to make them even more deadly. That is also irrefutably true, as will be explained below. She then makes other claims that could be true or could be misleading based on human bias.

However, the entire *Plandemic* controversy was a red herring or distraction from getting at the truth. We do not need the testimony of Judy Mikovits to know that the NIH and U.S. Army do indeed create manmade dangerous viruses. Tony Fauci admitted to this in a 2011 Op-Ed in the

---

[12] The Biological Weapons Convention (BWC) is a legally binding treaty that outlaws biological arms

Washington Post. It is worth reading in its entirety. The following is an excerpt:

"A flu virus risk worth taking

By Anthony S. Fauci, Gary J. Nabel, and Francis S. Collins
The Washington Post. December 30, 2011

...Two recent studies co-funded by the National Institutes of Health have shed light on how this potentially grave human health threat could become a reality. **Working carefully with influenza viruses they have engineered in isolated biocontainment laboratories**, scientists in Europe and the United States have identified several mechanisms by which the virus might evolve to transmit efficiently in the ferret, the best animal model for human influenza infection. This research has allowed identification of genetic pathways by which such a virus could better adapt to transmission among people. **This laboratory virus does not exist in nature**. There is, however, considerable concern that such a virus could evolve naturally. We cannot predict whether it or something similar will arise naturally, nor when or where it might appear.

Given these uncertainties, important information and **insights can come from generating a potentially dangerous virus in the laboratory**...

Understanding the biology of influenza virus transmission has implications for outbreak prediction, prevention and treatment. In defining the mutations required for mammalian transmission, public health officials are provided with genetic signatures that, like fingerprints, could help scientists more readily identify newly emergent, potentially harmful viruses, track their spread and detect threatening outbreaks. The ability to identify such viruses even a few months faster than by conventional surveillance provides critical time to slow or stop an outbreak. For example, the CDC implements public health protective measures and stockpiles antiviral drugs. Identifying threatening viruses can also facilitate the early stages of manufacturing vaccines that protect against such a virus in advance of an outbreak.

In addition, determining the molecular Achilles' heel of these viruses can allow scientists to identify novel antiviral drug targets that could be used to prevent infection in those at risk or to better treat those who become infected. Decades of experience tells us that disseminating information gained through biomedical research to legitimate scientists and health officials provides a critical foundation for generating appropriate countermeasures and, ultimately, protecting the public health.

The question is whether benefits of such research outweigh risks…

Along with support for this research comes a responsibility to ensure that the information is used for good. **Safeguarding against the potential accidental release or deliberate misuse of laboratory pathogens is imperative**. The engineered viruses developed in the ferret experiments are maintained in high-security laboratories. The scientists, journal editors and funding agencies involved are working together to ensure that access to specific information that could be used to create dangerous pathogens is limited to those with an established and legitimate need to know."

So, in that deceptive and rambling Op-Ed above, what Tony Fauci and his boss, Francis Collins, were really describing, without actually naming it, was the highly unethical process known as "gain-of-function" creation of viruses that do not occur in nature. Gain-of-function is a euphemism for "make a virus deadlier".

Most scientists condemn the practice.[13] Well then, how and why did the NIH get into the business of playing god if the scientific community condemns it?

Likely after years of secret military gain-of-function testing at Fort Detrick and elsewhere that never made it into the press, Tony Fauci's NIAID started to officially create viruses (i.e. WMDs) shortly after his 2011 Op-Ed. Then, in 2014, "after a string of high-profile biocontainment blunders in the US, including the accidental exposure of workers at the Centers for Disease Control and Prevention (CDC) to anthrax[14], and a dangerous mishandling of avian flu samples[15], which saw a deadly strain unintentionally substituted for a benign sample"[16], President Obama shut down the Fauci/Collins pet projects and ordered a review. Ebola also became an epidemic in Africa and spread to the

[13] Edelmann A, et al. "Disparate foundations of scientists' policy positions on contentious biomedical research" Proceedings of the National Academy of Sciences (PNAS) first published May 30, 2017 https://doi.org/10.1073/pnas.1613580114

[14] "CDC Lab Incident: Anthrax" CDC website. July 19, 2014

[15] "CDC Director Releases After-Action Report on Recent Anthrax Incident; Highlights Steps to Improve Laboratory Quality and Safety" CDC website. July 11, 2014.

[16] Dockrill P. "The US Just Ended Its Own Ban on Engineering Deadly Viruses in The Lab" Science Alert blog. https://www.sciencealert.com December 20, 2017.

U.S. in 2014, which is another virus allegedly made by man.[17], [18]

In 2016, a "white paper" commissioned by the NIH (to whitewash their past mistakes and make it seem as if the NIH was being safe and cautious going forward) was published.[19] However, this report made no conclusions at all, really, other than laying out commonsense vague guidelines on how to go about risking a deadly pandemic while pretending to be ethical in the process. In classic federal government style, it served to cover all the bases (or cover bureaucrats' arses) and equivocated.

Then, in December of 2017, at the peak of dysfunction and confusion amidst the inexperienced new Trump administration, which was distracted by the Russian-collusion probes, the NIH somehow sneaked back into the deadly-virus-creation business by lifting the hold. The HHS issued *Framework for Guiding Funding Decisions about Proposed Research Involving Enhanced Potential Pandemic Pathogens*.[20] Francis Collins issued a statement too.[21] Of course, these guidelines were so confusing, establishing layer upon layer of oversight committees, that any potential future blame for a lab

---

[17] Mikovits J, et al. "Plague: One Scientist's Intrepid Search for the Truth about Human Retroviruses and Chronic Fatigue Syndrome (ME/CFS), Autism, and Other Diseases" Skyhorse Publishing. February 21, 2017

[18] Mikovits J, et al. "Plague of Corruption: Restoring Faith in the Promise of Science (Children's Health Defense)" Skyhorse Publishing. June 2, 2020

[19] Selgelid M. "Gain-of-Function Research: Ethical Analysis" Sci Eng Ethics. 2016; 22(4): 923–964.

[20] "Framework for Guiding Funding Decisions about Proposed Research Involving Enhanced Potential Pandemic Pathogens" HHS website "Public Health Emergencies" https://www.phe.gov 2017

[21] Collins F. "NIH Lifts Funding Pause on Gain-of-Function Research" NIH website https://www.nih.gov December 19, 2017.

accident that might cause a global pandemic would be obscured and impossible to pin on Tony Fauci or Francis Collins.

Note that this HHS report gave gain-of-function the entirely new euphemism of "Enhanced Potential Pandemic Pathogens" and obscured the truth even further by shortening it to the acronym, "Enhanced PPP". By now, even scientists in the field were totally thrown off course. *Enhanced PPP* sounds like a luxury sportscar upgrade rather than a WMD. "These aren't the droids you're looking for."

But the watered-down feckless 2017 guidelines of the HSS were further corrupted when the oversight and review process was done behind closed doors, not transparently as originally promised. In 2019, *Science* reported[22] that the same two virus labs in Wisconsin and the Netherlands, that allowed the mishaps causing the 2014 hold on research, were allowed to restart gain-of-function lab work without the public being made aware. That prompted another *Washington Post* Op-Ed on the topic.[23] This time, scientists were opposing the work.

Why was the Deep State of the NIH and military so motivated to keep this risky gain-of-function research alive? In the 2011 Fauci Op-Ed, they claimed that the vital purpose of the research was to know the genetic structure future possible pathogens in order to track their spreads

---

[22] Kaiser J. "EXCLUSIVE: Controversial experiments that could make bird flu more risky poised to resume" Science. February 8, 2019.
[23] Lipsitch M, et al. "The U.S. is funding dangerous experiments it doesn't want you to know about" The Washington Post. February 27, 2019.

earlier in an epidemic. However, that rationale does not pass the laugh test. It is a joke.

In the same essay, the bureaucrat duo let the cat out of the bag by writing, "[gain-of-function experiments] can allow scientists to identify novel antiviral drug targets that could be used to prevent infection in those at risk or to better treat those who become infected." Ah, now it makes sense. The HHS and its subdivisions, which have too many financial conflicts of interest with Big Pharma to list here, were enthralled at getting into the highly profitable antiviral drug development business. After all, Tony Fauci landed his job at the NIH in the 1980's by working on the AIDS epidemic and being involved in those early drugs. We will discuss these conflicts later on.

Why is the military involved in gain-of-function work being performed in high-containment labs located on bases, such as Fort Detrick? The military is infamous for sloppy inept management. Wasn't the CDC created to handle all matters related to epidemics? One can only presume that our military is working on measures and countermeasures for a possible biological war, just as Russia and China are doing.

After the 2014 laboratory accidents, the military issued a report based on a Department of Defense (DOD) Inspector General report.[24] The Government Accountability Office (GAO) issued its own report on all of the high-containment labs spread across the CDC, NIH, and military.[25] The results were shocking to the scientific

---

[24] "Evaluation of DoD Biological Safety and Security Implementation" Department of Defense Inspector General website. April 27, 2016.
[25] "HIGH-CONTAINMENT LABORATORIES: Comprehensive and Up-to-Date Policies and Stronger Oversight Mechanisms Needed to Improve Safety: GAO website. https://www.gao.gov/products/GAO-18-145 October 19, 2017.

community. Mistakes occurred frequently and nothing was done to prevent future mistakes.

For example,

"In 2015, a DOD lab triggered a much larger emergency. Workers at the Dugway Proving Ground, an Army facility in Utah, shipped live anthrax to 194 laboratories instead of sending safely inactivated organisms that could not cause infection. The dangerous pathogens arrived in at least one lab in every state and nine facilities in other countries, according to the new DOD assessment.

Making the mistake more egregious, the anthrax shipments were intended only for testing detection equipment, not for research, and so were sent to labs that would not have been equipped to handle the live organism.

The errors did not cause anyone to become infected, but they triggered criticism by prominent scientists and scrutiny from Congress and the White House, as well as calls to shut down select-agent research in the U.S."[26]

Based on these ongoing safety risks at U.S. high-containment labs, it is not difficult at all to imagine that the Wuhan lab in China had an accident and the coronavirus leaked into the population. However, what is indeed hard to believe, mind boggling actually, is that Tony Fauci's NIAID funded the foreign lab work in Wuhan, China.

Say what? Yep. That really happened.

[26] McKenna M. "Military Labs Are Too Careless With Deadly Diseases: Report" National Geographic website. May 6, 2016.

> "The NIH research consisted of two parts. The first part began in 2014 and involved surveillance of bat coronaviruses, and had a budget of $3.7 million. The program funded Shi Zheng-Li, a virologist at the Wuhan lab, and other researchers to investigate and catalogue bat coronaviruses in the wild. This part of the project was completed in 2019. A second phase of the project, beginning that year, included additional surveillance work but also gain-of-function research for the purpose of understanding how bat coronaviruses could mutate to attack humans."[27]

So far, we have painted a picture of classic government incompetence that led to a pandemic. It is a story of negligence but not malice. But what if the Wuhan virus was intentionally created in these labs for the express purpose of killing people? Well, that would be an entirely different drama that could cause a war.

Judy Mikovits, PhD has already gone on the record accusing the government of doing just this. We know that she was arrested at the direction of the NIH and has been the subject of a concerted smear campaign ever since. However, if one does not believe Dr. Mikovits, then maybe Chinese virologist, Dr. Li-Meng Yan, is credible.

Dr. Yan stated in an interview, "The genome sequence is like a human finger print…So based on this

---

[27] Guterl F. "Dr. Fauci Backed Controversial Wuhan Lab with U.S. Dollars for Risky Coronavirus Research" Newsweek website. April 28, 2020

you can identify these things."[28] She then published a highly credible scientific paper detailing the exact reasons that the Wuhan virus genome is not like that of a naturally occurring virus and, instead, looks like an engineered virus.

> "The evidence collectively suggests that the furin-cleavage site in the SARS-CoV-2 Spike protein may not have come from nature and could be the result of genetic manipulation. The purpose of this manipulation could have been to assess any potential **enhancement of the infectivity and pathogenicity of the laboratory-made coronavirus. Evidently, the possibility that SARS-CoV-2 could have been created through gain-of-function manipulations at the WIV is significant and should be investigated thoroughly and independently."** [29]

So, this is literally "Tony's virus". Anthony Fauci and Francis Collins first fought hard to normalize an illegal bioweapons research program in this country despite numerous lab accidents and safety risks serving as warnings. Then, he opened the equivalent of a Kentucky Fried Chicken franchise in Wuhan, China and had them create viruses away from American HHS scrutiny. The escape and spread of the SARS-CoV-2 coronavirus was not some one-in-a-million rare event. It was highly predictable and likely.

---

[28] Mucumici N. "Chinese virologist claims she has proof COVID-19 was made in Wuhan lab" NY Post website. September 11, 2020

[29] https://zenodo.org/record/4028830#.X2AI1YspCh-

Tony Fauci, among others, are to blame. He owns this. The Great Scamdemic of 2020 shut down the healthcare systems and economies of much of the world. It will take decades to assess the true impact of this man-made catastrophe.

Chapter 2: The Genie is Let Out of the Lab Bottle

Once the bungling humans in the Wuhan lab allowed the SARS-CoV-2 coronavirus to escape into the general population, it spread around the globe, just as most regular influenza cases do every year.[30,31] For whatever reason, China seems to be a breeding ground for pandemics (making Tony Fauci's decision to outsource their gain-of-function work to China even more inexcusable).

The first reported accounts of the viral outbreak came at the end of December, 2019 when Chinese-based journalists reported a few dozen cases of atypical pneumonia in Wuhan. However, some believe that the virus was released earlier.[32] In a statement, the government downplayed it as a "preventable and controllable" disease.[33] The Chinese government continued to allow citizens to freely fly around the world.[34]

On January 11, 2020, Chinese state media reported the first death.[35] The misinformation teams were in high

---

[30] "A Timeline of COVID-19 Developments in 2020" AJMC website. July 3, 2020

[31] Taylor D. "A Timeline of the Coronavirus Pandemic" New York Times website. August 6, 2020

[32] Gander K. "Some Scientists Think COVID-19 May Have Been Spreading Far Earlier than Previously Thought" Newsweek website. May 6, 2020

[33] Colarossi N. "8 times world leaders downplayed the coronavirus and put their countries at greater risk for infection" Business Insider website. April 11, 2020

[34] Bowden E. "China, WHO could have helped prevent COVID-19 pandemic: congressional report" The New York Post website. September 21, 2020

[35] Qin A, et al. "China Reports First Death From New Virus" New York Times website. January 10, 2020

gear as the communist state emphasized that the virus could not be spread from human to human and that it was infecting people who ate exotic small mammals like bats from "wet markets".

Within a week, the virus was being reported by the W.H.O.[36] to be in Japan and South Korea. Then, the United States reported its first case in a man who returned to Seattle from Wuhan.[37]

On January 23rd, China locked down the entire city of Wuhan with a population of 11 million.[38] However, due to the delay, an estimated 5 million Wuhan citizens had already fled the city. This was the first indication to the world that lockdowns are impossible to enforce and ineffective.

The W.H.O. remained in propaganda mode and did not issue any warnings until January 30th when it declared a global health emergency. "The declaration "is not a vote of no confidence in China," said Tedros Adhanom Ghebreyesus, the W.H.O.'s director-general. "On the contrary, the W.H.O. continues to have confidence in China's capacity to control the outbreak.""[39]

Promptly the next day, on January 31st, President Trump suspended direct flights into the U.S. for most people who had recently visited China.[40] However, it was

---

[36] World Health Organization. "Novel coronavirus (2019-nCOVID)" website. January 20, 2020

[37] Rabin R. "First Patient With Wuhan Coronavirus Is Identified in the U.S." NY Times website. January 21, 2020

[38] Qin A, et al. "Wuhan, Center of Coronavirus Outbreak, Is Being Cut Off by Chinese Authorities" NY Times website. January 22, 2020

[39] Wee SL, et al. "W.H.O. Declares Global Emergency as Wuhan Coronavirus Spreads" NY Times website. January 30, 2020

[40] Corkery M, et al. "Trump Administration Restricts Entry Into U.S. From China" NY times website. January 31, 2020

still easy to enter the U.S. by either lying to airport screeners or rigging flight itineraries. Nevertheless, it was the first move by any world leader to attempt controlling the spread. He was bucking the trend and showing leadership.

Then, the Democrats' knee-jerk reaction of criticizing Trump for everything betrayed them. Speaker of the House Nancy Pelosi immediately took to Twitter on January 31st to condemn Trump's travel ban,

> "The Trump Admin's expansion of its un-American travel ban is a threat to our security, our values and the rule of law. Barring more than 350 million people from predominantly African countries from traveling to the US, this rule is discrimination disguised as policy."

On February 4th, she sat behind the president at the State of the Union Address, without a mask, gloating in her recent petty accomplishment of impeaching Trump in her House chamber (which was promptly tossed out in the Senate trial), completely unconcerned about the Wuhan virus. Senator Chuck Schumer and New York Mayor Bill de Blasio visited New York's Chinatown on February 9th to proclaim it safe.[41] Nancy Pelosi then visited her own Chinatown in San Francisco on February 24th, three-weeks after the W.H.O. declared an emergency, and declared it safe to visit. ""That's what we're trying to do today is to say everything is fine here," Pelosi said. "Come because

[41] Keleshian K. "Thousands Attend Chinatown New Year Parade In Show Of Unity Amid Virus Fears" WCBS radio website. February 9, 2020

precautions have been taken. The city is on top of the situation."'"[42]

Keep in mind that Tony Fauci was still an unknown name to the public at this point. He had not yet weighed in.

On February 4th, the first death outside of China was reported in the Philippines. The next day, a Japanese cruise liner was quarantined. The global death tool (assuming China was not lying and grossly underreporting) was 360. On February 7th, a Chinese doctor named Dr. Li Wenliang sounded the alarm and was persecuted by the government. He then died from the virus. On February 11th, the W.H.O. created the propaganda term COVID-19, as detailed in the first chapter.

In the second half of February, European nations got hit, first in France and then in Italy. The Italian government locked down 10 towns. Days later, Iran became a hot spot. Italy was more accessible to the press than Iran and the overburdened hospitals with people in the hallways shocked the world.

On February 29th, the first U.S. death as reported. As mentioned, the Seattle man had come back from a trip to Wuhan, China. It was later realized that an entire Seattle nursing home, the Life Care Center of Kirkland, had been infected with a large portion of the residents eventually abandoned to die as outside medical care was cut off due to a quarantine of the facility. President Trump raised the threat level of his travel ban to "do not travel" for Italy and South Korea.

Around this time, Tony Fauci started to rise in the news giving policy advice during rogue interviews. The

---

[42] "Nancy Pelosi Visits San Francisco's Chinatown Amid Coronavirus Concerns" NBC Bay Area TV website. February 25, 2020

Stock Market Crash of 2020 happened in the week of March 2nd.

On March 3rd, the CDC began PCR testing programs. On March 7th, more PCR-positive cases were reported in New York City. A Johns Hopkins website portal became the official source of information on total cases and deaths around the world and the press began the daily case count, largely ignoring the fact that the sensitive PCR tests were picking up RNA pieces as the person tested remained totally asymptomatic. Nerveless, case-mania dominated the news as the fear grew.

All of this led to Governor Andrew Cuomo issuing a state of emergency on March 7th. The order was aimed at helping hospitals with equipment. There was no discussion of taking away liberties of the people, banning indoor dining, closing restaurants, or requiring masks be worn.

The weeks of March 2nd and March 9th were eerie times. This author had landed in New York City on Sunday, March 8th for an oral argument in the Second Circuit Court of Appeals. The court had denied a motion to conduct it by telephone. Government buildings and the private sector were still open. Americans had never worn masks in public unlike Asia. Almost no one was wearing a mask. But people were on edge. Hand sanitizers started to appear in lobbies of hotels, for example.

The brush was dry and the wildfire was about to ignite. Then, Supreme Leader Tony lit the match.

On March 11th, Tony Fauci shut down most of the global economy with just a few unsubstantiated words of opinion during a congressional briefing.

The Wall Street Journal wrote,

"Just two days ago, when a Republican congressman used his time in a public coronavirus briefing to ask a top U.S. health official about sports, he thought he would get a calming response. The Ivy League had recently canceled the rest of its season. The National Basketball Association was still playing in full arenas.

...The unsettling answer that Dr. Anthony Fauci offered to Congress changed everything over a dizzying 24 hours that will be remembered as the most extraordinary day for American sports in decades.

"We would recommend that there not be large crowds," said Fauci, the director of the National Institute of Allergy and Infectious Diseases, an expert who has been a fixture of American public health for nearly four decades. "If that means not having any people in the audience when the NBA plays, so be it."

Fauci's candid remarks caught the NBA and some Trump administration officials by surprise."[43]

After those comments, the NBA shut down and the rest of the global sporting world followed suit. The power of fear from an invisible enemy was so strong that other industries toppled like dominos. Within a month, 30 million Americans had lost their jobs. 20.5 million jobs vanished in April alone, which is a number never seen before. Even after the Great Depression of 2008, job losses were under 1 million per month.

On March 13th, Trump issued a national emergency and assembled his pandemic response team. On March 15th,

[43] Cohen B, et al. "How a Doctor, Congressman and NBA Star Shut Down American Sports" WSJ website. March 13, 2020

the lockdowns began. The CDC recommended that no large gatherings over 50 people be held, but with no scientific basis to support the policy. It prompted New York City to close schools, and the rest of the nation followed. California issued stay-at-home (i.e. house arrest) orders on March 19th.

However, those initial social-distancing guidelines issued by The White House, approved by the Three Stooges of Fauci, Birx, and CDC Director Robert Redfield, were only supposed to last for 15-days.[44] The goal was to "flatten the curve", as Tony repeated over and over in his polyp-hoarse voice and Brooklyn accent. Then, like the Iraq War, the government overreach extended for more than six-months.

On March 17th, The Trump administration expanded telehealth allowing doctors to treat across state lines. It also increased reimbursement to the same levels as in-person visits. $1,200 direct checks went out to most Americans regardless of employment.

By this time, several cruise ships off the California coast were being held out to sea due to positive cases. They became unintentional clinical trials of the virus in terms of virulence, death rate, and symptomology. The aircraft carrier Theodore Roosevelt also suffered an outbreak resulting in the firing of the captain.

On March 27th, President Trump managed to have the divided congress pass an economic relief bill that provided loans and grants to people put out of work.[45]

---

[44] "15 Days to Slow the Spread" The Whit House website. March 16, 2020

[45] The Relief and Economic Security (Cares) Act

Subsequent extensions of the plan all totaled more than $3 trillion, which increased the national debt to unsafe levels.

President Trump's daily briefings were the most viewed show on TV for many weeks. He turned them into a reality TV show with a cast of characters in his entourage, such as Scarf-Woman Dr. Deborah Birx and the diminutive Tony Fauci playing the part of Omarosa as Trump's enemy. Given the stress of the impeachment stunt and the Russian Collusion hoax, a highly-rated TV show must have been a welcomed respite for the showman.

Soon, the reality show jumped the shark and Trump cancelled it, but not before the world witnessed the so-called experts flip-flop on several major guidelines. First, the White House response team mocked anyone who wanted to wear a mask, saying they were ineffective. Then, they mandated masks. They lied to our faces, as will be detailed late.

Tony Fauci stood next to HHS Secretary Alex Azar and the CDC's Redfield to state that, "The one thing historically that people need to realize that, even if there is some asymptomatic transmission, in all the history of respiratory borne viruses of any type, asymptomatic transmission has never been the driver of outbreaks. The driver of outbreaks is always a symptomatic person." A W.H.O. doctor said something similar. "Maria Van Kerkhove, PhD, head of the W.H.O. emerging diseases and zoonosis unit, said that though a person with COVID-19 who is not showing symptoms can spread the virus, "it still seems to be rare."" [46] However, those assertions conflicted

[46] Vaidya A, et al. "Asymptomatic COVID-19 cases not driving virus' spread, WHO officials say: 4 things to know" Becker's Hospital review website. June 8, 2020

with the Trump-resistance goal of lockdowns. So, Fauci reversed himself and the W.H.O. discredited their own senior scientist.

Tony Fauci flip-flopped on therapies too. He was initially in favor of using hydroxychloroquine (HCQ) and then said it was ineffective and dangerous. The FDA first approved HCQ for emergency use and then rescinded it.

By this time, the Great Scamdemic had been fully put into action. Science had become hijacked by the propaganda teams. Nothing in the mainstream news was reliable without verification.

By exploiting the fear, the Democrats saw the destruction of Trump's economy as the only way to win the presidential election in November. The few genuine hot spots in the country, such as Brooklyn, were portrayed in the press as representing the same level of outbreak threat to the rest of the country.

Despite being from Brooklyn, Tony Fauci never stepped foot in New York during the height of the crisis when thousands were dying each day in poorly managed hospitals and nursing homes. But that did not stop him from making headline news with his bold doomsday predictions.

Chapter 3: The Rise of Supreme Leader Tony

Tony Fauci, MD, was born in Brooklyn, New York on December 24th, 1940. Pearl Harbor had not happened and the U.S. was not fighting in WW2. Franklin Delano Roosevelt was president. A loaf of bread was ten cents and a car cost $800. Most forms of modern surgery and medicine had not yet been invented.

His father was Stephen Fauci, Sicilian and Catholic, and his mother was Eugenia Abys, Jewish of Swiss descent. His parents ran a pharmacy. "The Faucis ran a neighborhood pharmacy at 13th Avenue and 83rd Street and lived in an apartment above. The whole family helped out in the business — his dad working in the back of the pharmacy while his mother and sister operated the register. Tony delivered prescriptions from the time he was old enough to ride a bike.

He was raised in a Catholic tradition, receiving his first communion at age 7 and confirmation at age 12. Strong family relationships were an important part of Tony's upbringing."[47]

When asked about his upbringing for interviews, Tony often references his high school days as an athlete. "In the 1950s Bensonhurst was a working-class Brooklyn neighborhood for Italians and Jews. You just didn't talk about your academic achievements. Tony became streetwise, which later would serve him well.

He was a strong athlete, playing basketball from fall to spring and baseball from spring to fall at Dyker Heights Park. Tony rooted for the New York Yankees, and his early heroes included Joe DiMaggio and Mickey Mantle. This made him something of an outcast among his friends, who were Brooklyn Dodger fans." *Id.*

Therefore, it must have been the disappointment of a lifetime when he badly botched the first pitch at the Washington Nationals baseball game in 2020, throwing the ball into the ground 30-degrees to the left of target. He was later seen in the stands violating his own social-distancing recommendations by sitting next to two people with his mask below his chin.

---

[47] Gallin J. "Introduction of Anthony S. Fauci, MD: 2007 Association of American Physicians George M. Kober Medal" J Clin Invest. 2007 Oct 1; 117(10): 3131–3135

Photo: Alex Brandon/Associated Press,
fair use doctrine

In 1962, Tony Fauci entered medical school at Cornell where he reportedly finished first in his class.[48] "In 1966, during the Vietnam War, he was called to serve. He left New York City for the National Institutes of Health (NIH) to join what was affectionately called the "Yellow Berets". He served his military obligation in the Public Health Service at NIH.

From 1970 to 1971 he left the NIH to serve as Chief Resident at the New York Hospital Cornell Medical Center. Tony Fauci returned to NIH in July 1971 as a Senior Investigator in the Laboratory of Clinical Investigation and rapidly passed his clinical board examinations in internal medicine, infectious diseases, and allergy/immunology, with top scores. He then began his extensive and

[48] This claim has not been confirmed. Tony Fauci ignored our interview requests.

uninterrupted career in public service, serving continuously in the government."[49]

The text above is from a glowing article that quoted a speech introducing Fauci during an awards banquet. By this time, Fauci was a very powerful man in academic medicine, controlling the purse strings for billions of dollars in NIH grants. The words sound much like what a subservient general in the North Korean army would say about their Supreme Leader Kim Jong-un.

In 1981, Tony's big career break came at the cost of millions of gay men suffering from a mystery illness later to be defined as AIDS. His lab discovered some key elements of the virus. In 1984, he became director of NIAID. He still holds that position 36-years later at age 80.

Note that Fauci is neither an epidemiologist nor mathematician. He was a cellular biologist many decades ago and has been a paper-pushing bureaucrat ever since. The importance of this will be explained shortly.

Tony Fauci also has no experience in policymaking or leadership outside of the NIH where he has worked his entire adult career. He has never been elected to anything. He has never worked outside of the federal government, which arguably makes him the least qualified person to be issuing calming leaderly advice to the world.

However, within the DC Bubble, Tony had been anointed long ago as the Czar of Viruses. Then, to the rest of the world, he was promoted in March of 2020 to "Supreme Leader Tony" status by the mainstream media thanks to his open disdain for the Evil Orange Man.

---

[49] Gallin J. "Introduction of Anthony S. Fauci, MD: 2007 Association of American Physicians George M. Kober Medal" J Clin Invest. 2007 Oct 1; 117(10): 3131–3135

It was Tony Almighty's off-the-cuff comments during the March congressional hearings that set off the global pandemic of fear. As previously mentioned in Chapter 2, his unsupported doomsaying related to the dangers of fans in sporting arenas led to nations around the world issuing edicts closing businesses that interacted with the public.

He got away with it unchallenged. What next could he do?

Supreme Leader Tony began to mock President Trump behind his back during the daily press conferences. He intentionally struck poses with crossed arms and rubbed his forehead in disgust, and he got away with it. Then, realizing that he had the full support of the StopTrump media behind him, Tony began to flagrantly contradict his own previous comments and not be discredited.

Was he in fact the most powerful man in the world rather than the president? Was he the tail wagging the dog?

On March 29th, during another rogue interview (he knew that the White House dared not stop him for fear of looking like they were muzzling the Virus Czar and covering up the truth), Tony told CNN that there could be up to 200,000 deaths in the United Sates from the Wuhan virus.[50] However, he had lowered his guess down from his initial wildly irresponsible estimate of 1 to 2 million, which was based on bogus models from the UK, as will be explained.

Tony's crying fire in a theater caused the president to extend the initial 15-day social distancing policy for another month, until the end of April. That led to states issuing their own orders of business closures and house arrest for much of the rest of the year.

---

[50] https://twitter.com/CNNSotu/status/1244275909944885248

Tony Fauci was clearly bluffing, pretending to base his estimates on some black-box mystery model, and this author was the first to say so publicly in an essay[51] and on New York radio.[52] I have experience at making predictive financial models for Wall Street and knew that Fauci could not possibly have a grasp of the variables needed to make an estimate on the outbreak. We did not even know the death rate from the virus at the time. Also, importantly, he has no training whatsoever in epidemiology, math, or modeling. He was, at the time, a 79-year-old career Deep State employee and former cell biologist three decades ago.

Via email, this author's Fauci interview went as follows:

"Dr. Fauci, I will be on national radio tomorrow. I need to know more about the methods you used to project 200,000 deaths. It is not enough to say that some magical black box formula predicts this. What are your assumptions and driving variables? Thank you."

Fauci replied by dodging my question and punting to Dr. Birx instead, "Dr. Greer: Dr. Birx has been utilizing a number of models including from Imperial College (London) and Chris Murray from the Institute for Health Metrics and Evaluation at the University of Washington in Seattle. The models indicate that there could be 100,000 to 200,000 deaths in the USA. Please remember, as I am sure you are aware, models are only as good as the assumptions that you put into the models. And so, the number that I gave was not a prediction, but a number based on models.

---

[51] Greer SE. "Tony Fauci is purely guessing when he estimates up to 200,000 people could die" GreerJournal.com April 1, 2020

[52] Piscopo J, Greer SE. "Joe Piscopo discusses the Wuhan virus with Steven E. Greer, MD- April 2, 2020" GreerJournal.com April 2, 2020

Dr Birx did the detailed analyses. Thanks. Best regards, Tony"

I replied, "Dr. Fauci, This does not answer my question. It reiterates the estimates you spoke about. I am asking you to explain how you derived these outlandish estimates of 200,000 deaths and shed light onto the magical black box you all are using. I am modeling this too. I am an excellent forecaster, having done it on Wall Street. I get 30,000 deaths, worst case scenario, if 40 Million are tested and we have a 5% positive rate. Is this your final non-answer; to dodge the question?

Also, I am going out on a limb here and assuming you have not stepped foot in New York for a long time. How then do you know why the Third-World hospitals in Queens are having such high death rates? Have you considered incompetency?" Tony Fauci stopped replying at this point.

Then, the actual death counts in May and June were looking to be a factor ten lower than the Imperial College model he relied upon. So, Birx and Fauci spun it as a victory explaining that "millions of lives were saved" by the lockdowns, and why not? They have gotten away with saying anything and not being checked by the media.

However, that model was made by one very unreliable man, "Professor Neil Ferguson, who led the COVID-19 modeling team at Imperial College in London, resigned May 5 from his government advisory role after breaking the very same British lockdown rules that he had a role in influencing. Ferguson led the Imperial College team that designed the computer model that, among others, had been used to justify the recent stay-at-home orders in England as well as in the United States. We now know the model was so highly flawed it never should have been relied upon for policy decisions to begin with."[53]

The CATO Institute reported on the Ferguson models:

"When it came to dealing with an unexpected surge in infections and deaths from SARS-CoV-2 (the virus causing COVID-19 symptoms), federal and state policymakers understandably sought guidance from competing epidemiological computer models. On March 16, a 20-page report from Neil Ferguson's team at Imperial College London quickly gathered enormous attention by producing enormous death estimates. Dr. Ferguson had previously publicized almost equally sensational death estimates from mad cow disease, bird flu and swine flu.

This worst-case simulation came up with 2.2 million deaths by simply assuming that 81% of the population gets infected –268 million people– and that 0.9% of them die. It did *not* assume health systems would have to be overwhelmed to result in so many deaths, though it did make that prediction.

Neither the high infection rate nor the high fatality rate holds up under scrutiny.

The key premise of 81% of the population being infected should have raised more alarms than it did. Even the deadly "Spanish Flu" (H1N1) pandemic of 1918–19 infected no more than 28% of the U.S. population. The next

---

[53] Kevin Dayaratna, Ph.D. "Failures of an Influential COVID-19 Model Used to Justify Lockdowns" The Heritage Foundation website . May 18, 2020

H1N1 "Swine Flu" pandemic in 2009-10, infected 20-24% of Americans."[54]

Regarding the Chris Murray modeling often cited on TV screens in the West Wing by Scarf-Woman, "One analysis of the IHME model found that its next-day death predictions for each state were outside its 95 percent confidence interval 70 percent of the time — meaning the actual death numbers fell outside the range it projected 70 percent of the time. That's not great! (A recent revision by IHME fixed that issue.)

This track record has led some experts to criticize the model. "It's not a model that most of us in the infectious disease epidemiology field think is well suited" to making projections about Covid-19, Harvard epidemiologist Marc Lipsitch." [55, 56]

Fauci then told the media, "You can't really rely on models.[57] But like a broken clock that is correct twice a day, Fauci's predictions based on those discredited models now seem to have been prescient as the "death count" in the U.S. reached 200,000 by September.

Wait. Not so fast. It turns out that states and hospitals are massively overdiagnosing "COVID-19" as the cause of death because the government pays them to do so,

---

[54] Reynolds A. "How One Model Simulated 2.2 Million U.S. Deaths from COVID-19" CATO website. April 21, 2020.

[55] Begley S. "Influential Covid-19 model uses flawed methods and shouldn't guide U.S. policies, critics say" STAT website. April 17, 2020

[56] Piper K. "This coronavirus model keeps being wrong. Why are we still listening to it?" Vox website. May 2, 2020

[57] Hoft J. "WOW! Dr. Fauci Now Says, "You Can't Really Rely Upon Models" ...WTH? Gateway Pundit website. April 3, 2020.

among other reasons. The government guidelines allow them to stated COVID as the death even without a test as verification. "Presumed" COVID is all that is required. Crime pays.

Minnesota State Senator Scott Jensen, MD said,

> "Hospital administrators might well want to see COVID-19 attached to a discharge summary or a death certificate. Why? Because if it's a straightforward, garden-variety pneumonia that a person is admitted to the hospital for – if they're Medicare – typically, the diagnosis-related group lump sum payment would be $5,000. But if it's COVID-19 pneumonia, then it's $13,000, and if that COVID-19 pneumonia patient ends up on a ventilator, it goes up to $39,000."[58]

So, once again, the Centers for Medicare & Medicaid Services (CMS) created a financial incentive that led to poor outcomes and harm (In a subsequent chapter, reforms needed to the entire HHS are detailed.). Also, is that why patients in New York hospitals controlled by Governor Cuomo were placing terminally ill patients on ventilators and then not properly monitoring them (to be detailed later)?

Subsequent chapters will detail further how audits have proven that state reporting of COVID-19 deaths have been inflated by 100-time. For example, in Collin County

---

[58] Rogers M. "Fact check: Hospitals get paid more if patients listed as COVID-19, on ventilators" USA Today website. April 24, 2020

Texas, 4,600 were corrected down to 100 deaths from COVID. The county posted on their COVID website,

> "Notice: Collin County is providing COVID-19 numbers and data as a convenience to our residents. However, Department of State Health Services (DSHS) officials have acknowledged that the active case count for Collin County is significantly overstated. We advise residents that Collin County lacks confidence in the data currently being provided to us. DSHS officials have agreed to immediately redirect resources to correct the issue, but have not provided a timeline on when their reports will be corrected."[59]

Back to Supreme Leader Tony, only many months later did the Wizard of Oz curtain start to slowly pull apart and expose the fraud behind it, Tony Fauci, but the damage was already done. The American healthcare system for most forms of routine care had been closed off to the public causing unknown deaths from misdiagnosed cancers, untreated dementia in nursing homes, etc. Many businesses were destroyed. Millions were put of work. Mental illness skyrocketed causing deaths from suicide and overdoses. Domestic violence increased,[60] and students were withheld the vital in-person school sessions that young brains need.

Many might believe that Supreme Leader Fauci was benevolently overreacting to err on the side of caution in

---

[59] Collin County, Texas website. August 24, 2020

[60] Evans M, et al. "A Pandemic within a Pandemic — Intimate Partner Violence during Covid-19" NEJM media release website. September 16, 2020

order to save lives. However, the evidence is to the contrary. Lockdowns caused unfathomable harm.

Led by Tony, the U.S. and most of the rest of the world did the exact opposite of what should have been done. The vulnerable were left out of needed quarantine while the rest of the population was needlessly quarantined. They violated the first principle of epidemiology.

Chapter 4: From Supreme Leader to Tony Virus

During an episode of the Joe Piscopo radio show on September 17th, I made a Freudian slip and called Tony Fauci "Tony Virus".[61] Piscopo joked that it would be a good nickname in a mafia movie, like, "Hey, here comes Tony Virus. Tony Virus, how ya'doin?"". So, the nickname shall live on because it is well deserved.

Mentioned above, Supreme Leader Tony knew that he had so much blind support from the StopTrump mainstream press that he could literally say anything and not be checked. His wild predictions based on nothing grew even more outlandish. He began to contradict his own words with impunity. First, this author began to mock him. Then, Twitter accounts joined in. Finally, the conservative mainstream press piled on. The Supreme Leader had fallen in status down to Tony Virus.

Gateway Pundit posted an interesting essay in which they listed all of the times that Tony Virus made incorrect statements.[62] Those accounts have been fact-checked and verified.

In January, with pre-Supreme-Leader status, the unknown Tony went on Newsmax to dispel the myth that the virus was a threat.[63] He said, "This is not a major threat for the United States, and this is not something that citizens of the United States right now should be worried about."

Boom. Game over. Right there, this book should end: Tony Fauci thoroughly disqualified himself. But we

---

[61] Greer SE. "Joe Piscopo interviews Steven E. Greer, MD: 9-17-2020" GreerJournal.com. September 17, 2020

[62] Hoft J. "It Should be Obvious by Now that Dr. Fauci Is Insane" Gateway Pundit website. September 17, 2020.

[63] https://twitter.com/newsmax/status/1246131288664408064?lang=en

live in an insane world where rational thought falls way below politics in the hierarchy of power. Nobody seemed to notice this first of many fire-able offenses.

On March 26th, Fauci coauthored an opinion essay in the New England Journal of Medicine with the Director of the CDC, Robert Redfield,

> "This suggests that the overall clinical consequences of Covid-19 may ultimately be more akin to those of a severe seasonal influenza (which has a case fatality rate of approximately 0.1%) or a pandemic influenza (similar to those in 1957 and 1968) rather than a disease similar to SARS or MERS, which have had case fatality rates of 9 to 10% and 36%, respectively."[64]

Again, like a broken clock, Fauci ended up being correct, but not before he flip-flopped a week later and strongly endorsed the actions of New York and California governors who ordered complete lockdowns as if this were an Ebola outbreak. By now, the Democrat party had taken over the messaging for the Deep State, which includes the NIH and CDC.

On March 20th, still the Supreme Leader, Tony jumped to the podium to correct President Trump who had just finished making optimistic comments about hydroxychloroquine. A reporter asked a question and Trump nicely asked Tony to answer. Fauci said, "You have to be careful when you say fairly effective."

---

[64] Fauci A, Redfield, et al, "Covid-19 — Navigating the Uncharted" NEJM website. March 26, 2020

However, on March 24th, Fauci stated on Philadelphia's AM 990 The Answer radio show,

> "Yeah, of course [I would prescribe chloroquine to a Wuhan virus patient], particularly if people have no other option. You want to give them hope. In fact, for physicians in this country, these drugs are approved drugs for other reasons. They're anti-malaria drugs and they're drugs against certain autoimmune diseases, like lupus. Physicians throughout the country can prescribe that in an off-label way. Which means they can write it for something it was not originally approved for. People do that all the time, and it really is an individual choice between the physician and his or her patient as to whether or not they want to do that." [65]

Also, Fauci was certainly aware of an important virology paper from 2005 that concluded:

"We report that chloroquine has strong antiviral effects on SARS-CoV infection of primate cells. These inhibitory effects are observed when the cells are treated with the drug either before or after exposure to the virus, suggesting both prophylactic and therapeutic advantage. In addition to the well-known functions of chloroquine such as elevations of endosomal pH, the drug appears to interfere with terminal glycosylation of the cellular receptor, angiotensin-converting enzyme 2. This may

[65] Transcript of radio segment. Breitbart website. March 25, 2020.

negatively influence the virus-receptor binding and abrogate the infection, with further ramifications by the elevation of vesicular pH, resulting in the inhibition of infection and spread of SARS CoV at clinically admissible concentrations."[66]

On March 9th, Fauci said that cruise ships were safe despite knowing they were the most dangerous thing anyone could do in public due to the elderly demographic and close quarters. Cruise liners have an infamous past of bacterial and viral outbreaks. They are floating petri dishes.

Nevertheless, Fauci stated, "If you are a healthy young person, there is no reason if you want to go on a cruise ship, go on a cruise ship."[67]

Soon thereafter, many cruise ships around the world were quarantined off shore, stranding thousands of people for months. Proper medical care was not provided. Darwin's survival of the fittest theory was being tested in an accidental clinical trial. But again, there was not an ounce of outrage from the mainstream press.

Around this time is when Tony began to rely upon the aforementioned bogus Ferguson models and singlehandedly placed the world in a state of panic by estimating millions of deaths would occur. Again, he kept his job. Not only did he keep his job, but he was promoted to Supreme Leader Tony status due to the panic and his perceived "expert virologist" status.

---

[66] Vincent M. "Chloroquine is a potent inhibitor of SARS coronavirus infection and spread" Virol J online. August 22, 2005

[67] Gollan D. "COVID-19 Travel Update: Fauci Says Cruising Is OK If You Are Healthy" Forbes website. March 9, 2020

On April 15th, clearly bad at doing interviews, prone to gaffes, Tony went on Snapchat to proclaim that it is safe to hook up with strangers via Tindr for sex.[68] This was after he had said that people should never even shake hands again.[69] The media outrage was nowhere to be found.

Meanwhile, the original lockdowns ordered by the White House, which were designed only to last for 15-days in order to "flatten the curve" and prevent hospitals from being overloaded, had been extended for another 30-days, as previously mentioned. It was later learned that this foolish unscientific plan was derived from a W.H.O. plan.[70] Despite the numerous rad flags about the reliability of the W.H.O. being in bed with communist China, our own so-called epidemic experts relied on it to destroy the economy and cause terrible harm. President Trump soon thereafter cut funding to the W.H.O.

Finally, members of congress began to challenge Supreme Leader Tony, but very gingerly. On May 12th during a senate hearing, Senator Rand Paul, a practicing medical doctor, said to Fauci, "I think we ought to have a little bit of humility in our belief that we know what's best for the economy…And as much as I respect you, Dr. Fauci, I don't think you're the end-all. I don't think you're the one person that gets to make a decision."

Fauci replied, "I have never made myself out to be the end all, and only voice in this. I'm a scientist, a

---

[68] Cost B. "Dr. Fauci endorses Tinder hookups 'if you're willing to take a risk'" NY Post website. April 15, 2020

[69] Woods A. "Dr. Fauci says Americans should never shake hands again due to coronavirus" NY Post website. April 9, 2020.

[70] "Non-pharmaceutical public health measures for mitigating the risk and impact of epidemic and pandemic influenza" World Health Organization website. October 2019.

physician, and a public health official. I give advice according to the best scientific evidence."

Tony then made yet another classic "Fuacian" doomsday comment about schools, "We really better be very careful, particularly when it comes to children, because the more and more we learn, we're seeing things the virus can do that we didn't see from the studies in China, or in Europe," Fauci said. "You're right, in the numbers that children, in general, do much much better than adults and the elderly, and particularly those with underlying conditions, but I am very careful and hopefully humble that I don't know everything about this disease, and that's why I'm very reserved in making broad predictions." Of course, he had not a scintilla of "science" upon which to base that reckless public comment, as will be detailed later.

On July 17th, during a Fuacian rogue interview, no longer being viewed as the Supreme Leader Tony by most sane people, and now simply seen as parody in the form of Tony Virus from Brooklyn, told PBS,

> "We've got to do the things that are very clear that we need to do to turn this around," He told PBS NewsHour. "Remember, we can do it. We know that when you do it properly, you bring down those cases. We've done it. We've done it in New York...New York got hit worse than any place in the world. And they did it correctly by doing the things that you're talking about," added Fauci, director of the National Institute of Allergy and Infectious Diseases — and a member of the White House coronavirus task force."

Of course, Tony Virus knew that the opposite was true, but he was pandering to the Democrat party that had long ago hijacked the virus response. He was fleeing for salvation under the umbrella of the party.

Starting at ground zero, which was this author telling Joe Piscopo on the radio[71], then the New York Post, and then congressman Steve Scalise and others, it was well known that Governor Cuomo caused the huge death rates in New York that were not even close to any other part of the country. Cuomo-controlled hospitals were the worst of the worst, killing people, as will be detailed later. Cuomo failed to quarantine the vulnerable elderly and instead did the opposite. He forced sick hospitalized patients back into nursing homes to infect others. The Department of Justice is investigating this nursing home massacre.[72]

On September 11th, Tony Virus spewed more propaganda designed to restore his status back to Supreme Leader. Knowing that continued economic shutdowns might help Joe Biden, he went before the epicenter of the academic far-left elite and told a bunch of Harvard doctors via webcast that the U.S. should be like Australia and stay locked down until 2021.[73]

The rise and fall of Anthony Fauci, from unknown Deep State bureaucrat, to the most powerful man in the world, and then back down again to being a discredited scientist and nothing but a political hack disgracing the medical degree he holds, will be debated for decades. The

---

[71] Greer SE, Piscopo J. "Joe Piscopo discusses the Wuhan virus with Steven E. Greer, MD- April 2, 2020" GreerJournal.com. April 2, 2020

[72] Greer SE. "Dr. Steven Greer's efforts lead to DOJ investigating governors for causing nursing home virus deaths" GreerJournal.com. August 29, 2020

[73] https://twitter.com/JordanSchachtel/status/1304470827933536256

story is still unfolding and reflection is impossible at this point. If President Trump wins reelection and this nation avoids a Marxist takeover, then the history books might be a little more accurate than if the opposite occurs.

Now, let us examine the facts and scientific evidence that shows how this was all a Great Scamdemic perpetrated by American-hating Marxist enemies and the Deep State that they control. Major lessons must be learned or else the invisible enemy will be unleashed upon us again in 2024.

Chapter 5: What was the Real Risk of the Wuhan Virus?

To be clear, the Wuhan virus outbreak was very deadly to many thousands of people around the world. The virus selectively attacks cells that have the ACE-2 receptor (likely a feature designed in by the "gain-of-function" wizards in Tony Fauci's labs, as detailed in Chapter 1), which is found on the endothelial lining of blood vessels, lung pneumocytes, and other cells.

When those blood vessels become damaged by cell necrosis, that triggers the blood clotting cascade.[74] As the blood stops flowing, delicate organs, such as the lungs, brain, kidneys, etc. stop working. The lung cells are also directly targeted by the virus leading to an inflammatory cascade that results in cell death.[75] That is why, for patients who recover, they often have lingering breathing problems, etc.

However, most people under the age of 60 seem to not have a high enough concentration of ACE-2 receptors to make them vulnerable to serious illness from the Wuhan virus, as will be explained. Kids are particularly resistant to infection due to low receptor gene expression, about half that of adults, in their nasal passages where the virus likes to enter the host.[76]

Even for those who are susceptible to the virus, such as the elderly or those otherwise sick from chronic

---

[74] Ackermann M., et al. "Pulmonary Vascular Endothelialitis, Thrombosis, and Angiogenesis in Covid-19" NEJM website. July 9, 2020

[75] Vaduganathan M., et al. "Renin–Angiotensin–Aldosterone System Inhibitors in Patients with Covid-19" NEJM website. April 23, 2020

[76] Bunyavanich, S. "Nasal Gene Expression of Angiotensin-Converting Enzyme 2 in Children and Adults" JAMA website. June 16, 2020

diseases, we have several therapies that should prevent the virus from replicating and the blood from clotting. Therefore, those vulnerable groups should not have died from the Wuhan virus the way they did. The high death rates in certain parts of New York City, for example, were mostly caused by human error, as will be explained later.

OK, some people seem to die quickly from the Wuhan virus and some just get the sniffles. What is the real risk of death from contracting the Wuhan virus, looking at the big picture?

Well, that is a very difficult question to answer because one needs to know how many people were infected and never showed any symptoms at all. Then, one needs to know how many people died as a result of the virus, and even that number is highly dubious due to malfeasance.

The best estimate of the risk of death from the Wuhan virus to the white human population is 0.3%.

That is based on a thorough study conducted in Iceland of 30,000 people.[77] To date, it is the only study to have properly screened patients with the right panel of antibody assays in order to get a reliable "test-positive" rate. If a study were to fail to detect people who were actually infected but asymptomatic (as most studies have done), then it would greatly inflate the death rate.

What does 0.3% death rate mean? Is that scary bad or insignificant? It has to be compared to other diseases.

---

[77] Gudbjartsson D.F., et al. "Humoral Immune Response to SARS-CoV-2 in Iceland" NEJM website. September 1, 2020

The CDC estimates that the influenza pandemic of 2018-2019 killed 34,000 people of the 35.5 million symptomatic illnesses, for a 0.1% death rate.[78] However, rarely is a test performed to verify the regular flu. So, more people certainly have died who had the flu than is being reflected in those CDC numbers.

Regardless, the Wuhan virus seems to be about as deadly as the flu. But the Wuhan virus numbers are highly skewed toward small subpopulations of the elderly or chronically ill, whereas the regular flu is much less so. This means that the Wuhan virus could very well be LESS deadly than the flu for the typical healthy person under age 60 or so.

Common sense also is an important clue. Are people dropping dead in the streets from the Wuhan virus? No. Are morgues and funeral homes backlogged across the nation? Only in New York City, at the peak of the outbreak in the Spring, did we see that. Are hospitals overflowing? No.

In contrast, past pandemics from genuinely deadly viruses did literally cause people to drop dead and pile up in the streets. The Spanish Flu of 1918 (an H1N1 virus like the 2009 swine flu outbreak) is this nation's best example.[79]

The Spanish Flu killed at least 10% of the people it infected, as opposed to only 0.3% for the Wuhan virus (or 3,333 percent more deadly). "An estimated 500 million people, or one-third of the world's population, became infected with this virus. The number of deaths was

---

[78] "Disease Burden of Influenza" CDC website

[79] "Influenza 1918" American Experience TV series on PBS.

estimated to be at least 50 million worldwide with about 675,000 occurring in the United States."[80]

It seemed to target the youngest and healthiest of people, in stark contrast to the Wuhan virus. Healthy male soldiers in their teens and twenties coming back from World War 1 were the first to die. A perfectly healthy person could turn blue in the face, start bleeding from the nose, and die within 24-hours.

Of note, they tried the mask thing back then too. It was concluded that cloth masks (just like most people wear today) were of no use in preventing the spread of the epidemic. People still died despite wearing masks back in 1918.[81]

With the Spanish Flu, young children under the age of five were vulnerable and often died. In stark contrast again, **virtually no child has died from the Wuhan outbreak.**

A July report listed a single pediatric death in Canada.[82] Another July report listed zero pediatric deaths in Finland and Sweden despite Sweden having no lockdowns like the rest of the world.[83] In the U.S., a September report by the American Academy of Pediatrics listed essentially zero deaths as well (i.e. "0" – 0.13%").[84] This could be the

---

[80] "1918 Pandemic (H1N1 virus)" CDC website. No date or author listed.

[81] Kellogg W. of the California State Board of Health. "Influenza, a Study of Measures Adopted for the Control of the Epidemic" California State Printing Office, 1919

[82] Flanagan R. "How deadly is COVID-19 for children? Here's what we know" CTV News website. July 14, 2020

[83] Soderpalm H. "Sweden's health agency says open schools did not spur pandemic spread among children" Reuters website. July 15, 2020

[84] "Children and COVID-19: State Data Report" AAP website. September 17, 2020

most important point to make given that schools have been arbitrarily shut down for a year.

Let's assume for the sake argument that children were indeed dying from the Wuhan virus, which they are not. What other infectious disease kill children? Every year, thousands of kids still die from preventable diseases, such as measles, mumps, rubella, pertussis, meningitis, and the flu (Kids are walking germ factories and commonly sicken teachers and adults, yet schools are never shut down. So, why are schools closed now?).

But none of those infectious diseases are among the leading causes of death. What parents should worry about are accidents, cancers, and homicides as the leading causes of death.[85]

Having established that the Wuhan virus is, at worst, as deadly as the regular flu, how does that compare to other causes of death? A CDC report[86] lists the causes of death as:

- Heart disease: 647,457
- Cancer: 599,108
- Accidents (unintentional injuries): 169,936
- Chronic lower respiratory diseases: 160,201
- Stroke (cerebrovascular diseases): 146,383
- Alzheimer's disease: 121,404
- Diabetes: 83,564
- **Influenza and pneumonia: 55,672**
- Nephritis, nephrotic syndrome, and nephrosis: 50,633
- Intentional self-harm (suicide): 47,173

[85] "Child Health" CDC website. No date or author listed.
[86] "Leading Causes of Death" CDC website. 2017

As one can see, the “invisible enem
viruses is way down on the list of things o
over before they go to bed each night wor
will wake up ever again. A bedtime pray
God, please don’t kill me by heart disease,
and also the Wuhan virus.”

With all of the irrefutable and calming facts above, what then is the Marxist propaganda media using as evidence to claim that the Wuhan virus is a massive pandemic affecting millions of people, warranting the stripping of our civil liberties? Is it all just a “casedemic” based on highly erroneous PCR testing?

In most cases, the onslaught of propaganda has been in the form of misleading headlines followed by an article with no meat to it. For example, this is a Washington Post headline as seen by the Apple iPhone news app on September 22, 2020.[87]

[87] Achenbach J, et al. “Rising coronavirus case numbers in many states spur warning of autumn surge” Wash Post website. September 22, 2020

However, when one read the actual story, it was just another casedemic propaganda story designed for fearmongering. There is no credible clinical data to support their narrative that the Wuhan virus is an out-of-control deadly disaster.

As another example, *The Atlantic* magazine, owned by the billionaire ex-wife of Steve Jobs, published the casedemic article with the title *What Young, Healthy People Have to Fear From COVID-19.*[88]

** This article originally misstated the fatality rate for COVID-19 patients under 35.*

We want to hear what you think about this article. Submit a letter t letters@theatlantic.com.

DEREK THOMPSON *is a staff writer at* The Atlantic, *economics, technology, and the media. He is the author of the podcast* Crazy/Genius.

Connect  Twitter

But the article simply lied. First, it inflated the risk of death by twenty-fold. They had to quietly post a correction, "*This article originally misstated the fatality rate for COVID-19 patients under 35.*"

Aside from that discrediting mistake, the crux of the article was a new and creative way to fearmonger. The author conceded that the death rates from the Wuhan virus were very low. However, he then argued that the Wuhan

---

[88] Thompson d. "What Young, Healthy People Have to Fear From COVID-19" the Atlantic website. September 8, 2020

virus leads to long-term disability in young people who did not quite have a serious acute illness from the virus.

The Atlantic stated:

"The reality is that, so far, COVID-19 has killed fewer children and teenagers than seasonal flu in a normal year, according to data compiled by the Centers for Disease Control and Prevention. A 25-year-old who contracts this disease is approximately 250 times less likely to die than an infected 85-year-old, according to the most sophisticated estimates of infection-fatality rates. For every 1,000 people infected with COVID-19 under the age of 35, the average expected death count is less than one. These facts might give you the impression that, as Atlas said, "it doesn't matter if younger, healthier people get infected." But it does. It *really* does. Here's why.

You might be used to thinking of 30-somethings as safe and seniors as at risk in this pandemic. But if a man in his 30s and a man in his 60s both contract COVID-19, it is more likely that the 30-something will develop a months-long illness than that the 60-something will die, according to this research.

More frightening than what we're learning now is what we cannot yet know: the truly long-term—as in, decades-long—implications of this disease for the body. "We know that hepatitis C leads to liver cancer, we know that human papillomavirus leads to cervical cancer, we know that HIV leads to certain cancers," Howard Forman, a health-policy professor at Yale, told James Hamblin and Katherine Wells of *The Atlantic*. "We have no idea whether having had this infection means that, 10 years from now, you have an elevated risk of lymphoma.""

So, the StopTrump propaganda is now stooping to making up stuff out of thin air. They are citing fraudulent statistics that have to be retracted. Also, they are quoting irresponsible so-called experts, a non-scientist "health policy expert" in this case, to hand-wring about the unknown and present it as a real risk.

By the way, the Howard Forman analogies of the Wuhan virus possibly leading to cancers like HIV and HPV are biologically implausible. Both of those viruses have mechanism that allow the virus to stay in the human host for the life of the host, thereby triggering cancers. There is no indication that a coronavirus of any kind does that.[89]

Those are just two examples of misleading reports that have created the casedemic withing the scamdemic. A subsequent chapter will delve into this further.

By now, any reader who keeps up with the news should be asking, "If the Wuhan virus is not deadly, then why did 200,000 people die?" The answer is that the death toll stats are completely bogus and driven by financial incentives, politics, and bad testing methods.

As mentioned previously in Chapter 2, CMS created the perverse incentive for hospital administrators to pressure doctors to list all deaths as "COVID-19" because they received $39,000 in bundled payments as opposed to the usual $5,000. As local governments begin to audit these death certificates, they are finding that the deaths attributed to the virus have been inflated 100-fold.

---

[89] Blackburn K. "7 viruses that cause cancer" MD Anderson Cancer Center website. 2018

The CDC also made it confusing as to how to classify deaths in the scamdemic era. In a guidelines report, the CDC stated, “In cases where a definite diagnosis of COVID cannot be made but is suspected or likely (e.g. the circumstances are compelling with a reasonable degree of certainty) it is acceptable to report COVID-19 on a death certificate as 'probable' or 'presumed.”[90] (In the final chapter, we will discuss reforms needed at the CDC).

In addition, the arbitrary mass-testing policy was probably the biggest cause of the inflated death stats. Swabbing millions of people and then running highly sensitive PCR tests accomplished nothing other than create a casedemic.

First, what is PCR testing? PCR is the acronym for Polymerase Chain Reaction. It can take a small fragment molecule of DNA or RNA and amplify it until it is detectable. If a non-functioning remnant of the Wuhan virus RNA is found on a patient and detected by PCR, it would be a false-positive test and mislead the patient into thinking they need to be quarantined. That is what is happening often.

Then, even if the real virus is detected by PCR, it does not mean that the person is infectious. Asymptomatic people do not spread respiratory viruses effectively enough to drive a pandemic. Asymptomatic people can rarely pass it on, but pandemics are driven by sick people coughing on other people, as will be explained below in the “Maskquerade” chapter.

This is how PCR testing has caused a casedemic of “COVID deaths” Currently, in almost all hospitals, every

---

[90] “Vital Statistics Reporting Guidance: Guidance for Certifying Deaths Due to Coronavirus Disease 2019 (COVID–19)” Report No. 3. CDC website. April, 2020

patient is tested for the Wuhan virus whether they are sick or not. We have established how the vast majority of people never become ill from the virus. Therefore, many people in the hospital for care unrelated to a viral illness will be labeled as "COVID patients". When they die from an unrelated illness, they are categorized as a death caused by the Wuhan virus.

In conclusion, this Wuhan virus pandemic was not anything more deadly than the regular flu season, for the population at large. People of school age are immune and have an infinitesimally small risk of even a minor illness. Young children do not transmit the virus to adult teachers.[91] Also, the vast majority of healthy adults are at very low risk of suffering a serious illness.

Certain vulnerable groups that did see deaths could have been saved if they had received proper treatment. Those vulnerable groups were also not protected properly by quarantine. We will discuss that in more detail next.

[91] Gilliam W. et al. "COVID-19 Transmission in US Child Care Programs" Pediatrics website. October 14, 2020

Chapter 6: The Nursing Home Massacres

By sheer coincidence, I might possibly have been the most qualified person in the country to understand soonest what was going on in nursing homes. As the scamdemic became politicized and governments were clearly botching the quarantines, I smelled a rat.

As part of a larger concierge practice, I have a wound care practice that treats the elderly in nursing homes. It is dirty work that few doctors wish to do. It falls on the opposite end of the spectrum from cushy plastic surgery or Wall Street. However, it was a topic of research for me during my surgery residency training 20-years ago and I find it fascinating to be able to take a massive festering gangrenous wound and close it with proper care.

Back in the late 1990's at New York University Medical Center, as I conducted my clinical wound therapy trials and enrolled patients from New York nursing homes, I saw how poor the medical care was in those facilities. I then started the first bedside wound care service that was staffed by medical doctors. The paradigm at the time was to send the elderly to a centralized wound care clinic only when things got really bad.

Because of that experience, I know that the elderly, even under the best of conditions, are often isolated and become disoriented from lack of social interactions. When New York Governor Cuomo started to mismanage the hospitals and nursing homes in March of 2020, I immediately became concerned.

On the Joe Piscopo radio show, I was the first one in the nation to raise concerns about the high death rates being reported and whether it was a manmade disaster. On April 2, 2020, I told listeners of the Piscopo show that the elderly in nursing homes are very vulnerable to isolation.[92] I had made an official proposal to the White House emergency response team and CMS to use telemedicine as a novel way of communicating with the quarantined elderly and the nursing staff, but my proposal was ignored. I stated on the radio,

> "So, I have reached out to the White House. I have a company with a very famous doctor who is already advising the White House, we've got this incredible team. We already have gadgets where you can do a remote pulse oximetry . . . to make a long story short, I think we can immediately start using telemedicine because doctors are afraid to go into nursing homes. The elderly are being quarantined in these nursing homes, and even if they're not sick, they've been cut off from society. So, we need to do telemedicine. We need to get them iPads, screens where they can talk to doctors or even family members. That's step number one, and I have a proposal to do that, and I'm waiting for them to get back with me."

Then, a month later on Piscopo, we discussed how the foreseeable slaughter became a reality.[93] I said,

---

[92] Greer SE, Piscopo J. "Joe Piscopo discusses the Wuhan virus with Steven E. Greer, MD- April 2, 2020" GreerJournal.com. April 2, 2020
[93] Greer SE, Piscopo J. "Joe Piscopo discusses the Wuhan virus pandemic with Steven E. Greer, MD" GreerJournal.com. May 4, 2020

> "The nurses, they're not capable of dealing with an infectious disease problem, and Governor Cuomo, to show that the hospital rates were going down, or whatever bureaucratic idiotic reason, forced infected people from the hospitals into the nursing homes. Of course, they spread the virus. Now, the total number of all New York deaths is at least 25% comprised of those from nursing homes. They are slaughtering people because and the news doesn't report on it. And that's the manslaughter. If you can intentionally send a deadly virus into a nursing home, knowing it's going to kill other people, someone has to go to jail for that."

It turned out that I was being too kind to Governor Cuomo. We now believe that the percentage of all New York deaths that were nursing home deaths was closer to 80%.[94]

However, because Cuomo went into cover-up mode, those true data have not been released.[95] The oft-cited New York nursing home death count of 6,500 is likely underreported and actually closer to 11,000.[96]

This culling of the elderly was a manmade tragedy. It was the direct result of Governor Cuomo's misguided pandemic policy that cleared hospital beds at all costs, even

---

[94] Roy A. "The Most Important Coronavirus Statistic: 42% Of U.S. Deaths Are From 0.6% Of The Population" Forbes website. May 26, 2020.

[95] Hogan B. "Cuomo admin accused of stonewalling over COVID-19 nursing home death tally" NY Post website. September 1, 2020

[96] Condon B. "New York's true nursing home death toll cloaked in secrecy" Associated Press website. August 11, 2020.

if it meant that those infected with the Wuhan virus would to be readmitted to nursing homes to knowingly spread the infection. Several other Democrat governors directly copied Cuomo, expanding this felonious massacre across state lines.

On March 25th, 2020, Governor Cuomo's office issued an executive order that stated,

> "no resident shall be denied re-admission or admission to the [nursing home] solely based on a confirmed or suspected diagnosis of COVID-19. [The order also said nursing homes and adult facilities were] "prohibited from requiring a hospitalized resident who is determined medically stable to be tested for COVID-19 prior to admission or readmission."[97]

That order has since been deleted from the official website of the governor.[98] Cuomo then began a several-month-long campaign to revise history and blame President Trump, but it was too late. The public could see through his lies. Too many newspapers had blamed Cuomo for the deaths.[99]

This author was the first person in the country to publicly state that what Governor did was tantamount to

---

[97] Perrett C. "Gov. Cuomo's controversial order requiring nursing homes to admit COVID-19 patients was reportedly removed from New York's health website" Business Insider via MSN.com website. May 27, 2020

[98] https://www.governor.ny.gov/executiveorders

[99] Michael Goodwin of the New York Post began a series of articles on April 21, 2020, shortly after I made New Yorkers aware of the problem. His first article was "Andrew Cuomo's coronavirus nursing home policy proves tragic" NY Post website. April 21, 2020

manslaughter.[100] Not only that, I specifically stated on Rudy Giuliani's podcast that the Department of Justice, his former job before becoming mayor, and not the State of New York policing bodies, should investigate.[101]

Shortly thereafter, members of congress, who are also guests on the same radio stations as I appear (i.e. WABC 770 and AM 970), took the baton and ran with it. Congressman Steve Scalise really championed the cause and demanded an investigation into Governor Cuomo.

On August 26th, the DOJ announced that it was investigating the nursing home deaths.[102] A few days later, the Wall Street Journal published the Op-Ed "Cuomo gets a nursing home inspection".[103] On September 4th, the FBI raided a Pennsylvania nursing home that had copied the Cuomo-doctrine of forcing infected elderly back into the nursing homes to kill others.[104] On September 25th, two V.A. nursing home employees were criminally indicted by a grand jury on charges, "stemming from their decision to combine two dementia units in March, packing residents who were COVID-19 positive into the same room with those who had no symptoms".[105]

---

[100] Greer SE. Piscopo J. "Joe Piscopo discusses the Wuhan virus pandemic with Steven E. Greer, MD- May 4, 2020" GreerJournal.com May 4, 2020

[101] Greer SE, Giuliani R. "Rudy Giuliani interviews Steven E. Greer, MD on his podcast TV show: May 15, 2020" GreerJournal.com May 15, 2020

[102] Greer SE. "Dr. Steven Greer's efforts lead to DOJ investigating governors for causing nursing home virus deaths" GreerJournal.com. August 26, 2020

[103] "Cuomo gets a nursing home inspection" WSJ website. August 28, 2020

[104] Golding B. "FBI, state authorities raid Pennsylvania nursing homes amid COVID-19 probe" NY Post website. September 4, 2020

[105] Richer A. "2 Charged for Handling of Virus Outbreak at Veterans Home" Associated Press. September 25, 2020

Stay tuned. After the printing of this book, more indictments will likely follow.

I am often asked the question of why Governor Cuomo made the fateful decision to pack nursing homes with infected patients. I have a few theories, but I am not sure that even Andrew Cuomo knows why he did it. I chalk it all up to the chaos taking place in Albany during the peak of the pandemic when fear was overriding reason.

One must recall that, at the time, the big concern was to "flatten the curve", thanks to Tony Virus promoting this concept. The world had seen biased reporting from Italy and their overflowing hospitals and patients dying in hallways. The influential leaders of the best medical centers in Manhattan were panicking and pressuring Albany to keep the sick barbarians at the gates of Brooklyn, Queens, etc.

It was under this climate of fear that Cuomo somehow thought it would make him look bad as a politician if images like the world saw from Italy were reported taking place in his own hospitals. He wanted at all costs to empty the hospitals and make room for the "surge" in cases, even it meant sending the elderly to their slaughter in nursing homes.

Numerous hospitals in New York, which happened to also be the locations of the hot spots of the outbreak, are under the direct control of the governor, and have been badly mismanaged for decades. They have been incompetent at handling routine medical care and were woefully unprepared for an epidemic. I wrote an essay on this in March.[106]

---

[106] Greer SE. "The New York virus death rates are too high. Why?" GreerJournal.com March 29, 2020

In addition to those factors, I believe that the Democrats really do subscribe to eugenics philosophies and view elderly as drains to society. They have no qualms with euthanasia. The "death panels" Sarah Palin made famous during the 2008 election are real. Look at how easily the various state health officials, who mimicked Cuomo, sent their elderly to their deaths. In all cases, they were far-left ideologues.

Dr. Rachel Levine, the transgender head of the Pennsylvania health department

But it gets worse for Governor Cuomo. Hand in hand with his administration's decision to intentionally mix infected elderly in with the uninfected was their highly political decision to ban the use of hydroxychloroquine for use against the Wuhan virus. We had therapies that could have saved people. Even among the most vulnerable elderly, few people should have died if they had received the proper medications. It was unprecedented for governors to get in between medical doctors and patients and ban a drug that had been approved for 50-years. This will be discussed more in a subsequent chapter.

Now, where does Tony Virus fit in with all of this? Despite all of the above mistakes made by New York being well known to anyone, ole Tony decided to join ranks with his fellow Democrats and praise New York as being the model for how to handle a pandemic.

During a September 23rd U.S. Senate hearing, Rand Paul, MD pointed out to Tony Virus that he had praised New York despite New York being the textbook example of what NOT to do during a pandemic.[107] However, by now Tony was not even attempting to be impartial and was fully on board with the Democratic party agenda for the upcoming election. No amount of factual evidence could sway ole Tony.

---

[107] Nelson s. "Fauci and Rand Paul clash over Cuomo, NY handling of COVID-19" NY Post website. September 23, 2020

Chapter 7: The High Death Rates in New York Hospitals

Just as my unusual career experiences made me ideally suited to spot the tragedy unfolding inside nursing homes, so too did they allow me to be the very first person to declare that the high death rates in New York hospitals were a unique "New York problem" caused by poor healthcare. As a surgery resident, when I was conducting my clinical wound trials 20-years ago, I moonlighted as a doctor in Wyckoff Heights Medical Center in Brooklyn. That was one of the hot spots for the outbreak in 2020. I have seen the atrocious care delivered by these Cuomo-state-run hospitals even during normal non-pandemic times. I detailed it all in an essay.[108] I knew that there was no way they were handling the Wuhan virus patients properly. Sadly, I was right.

On April 9th, I told Joe Piscopo and his audience:

"Now, because of politics, Governor Cuomo is actually making it harder to get hydroxychloroquine. I think in the hotspots of these Queens hospitals, where people are dying by the thousands each day, I think a lot of them are not getting these medicines when there's plenty of medicine to go around, and if that's true—and if I find that out—that's going to be a big story.

Um, because all of the deaths across the nation . . . it's easy to look at the numbers, but it's really not that simple. It's where these numbers are coming from. They're

[108] Greer SE. "Coronavirus is a New York problem, not a national problem" GreerJournal.com. April 19, 2020.

being skewed by one or two hospitals in Queens. And so, it's very unrepresentative. The actual national death rate is much, much lower and it's because of the care they're getting…

It would not surprise me if you go to Elmhurst Hospital, Wycoff Hospital where they've got 1,000 people dying a day, that they're not getting hydroxychloroquine. It wouldn't surprise me…

I was the person who said ventilators are a red herring, a distraction of the political game. "How can we blame Trump and all that stuff?" The ventilators are too late. By the time you're on it, you've got acute respiratory distress syndrome, and, like you said, 86% die. That's not going solve this. We need to get millions and millions and millions of doses of these drugs out to everybody, and then, of course, a vaccine."[109]

On April 16th, I echoed those comments on One American News.[110]

At that same time, early in the outbreak, the world was praising hospital workers only as heroes. Therefore, I received some hostile pushback when I challenged that tenet.

To be clear, the vast majority of these hospital workers were indeed heroes who went to work knowing that they were literally risking their lives. They saw patients dying and were not given adequate protective gear. We knew little about the real virulence of the virus. This was a

---

[109] Greer SE, Piscopo J. "Joe Piscopo discusses the coronavirus with Steven E. Greer, MD- April 9, 2020" GreerJournal.com. April 9, 2020
[110] Greer SE. "Steven E. Greer, MD on OANN discussing virus therapies" GreerJournal.com. April 16, 2020

genuine pandemic as far as we all knew at the time. Therefore, for them to still go to work was the dictionary definition of heroism.

But then strange reports by visiting nurses from other states, where the healthcare delivered to Wuhan virus patients was much different, began to be posted online. In video testimonials, they detailed the horrors they witnessed in New York hot spot hospitals. An April 27th Daily Mail article detailed the scandal.[111] A second nurse came forward as well.[112]

At Elmhurst Hospital, Wyckoff Heights Medical Center, etc., the administrators of the hospitals had instructed there to be separate hospice wards, essentially, for the sick patients on ventilators. However, the two concepts of giving someone a highly-advanced form of medical care via a ventilator and providing only palliative hospice care are diametrically opposed. Of course, as mentioned in previous chapters, we now know why this insanity arose. It was part of a Medicare/Medicaid fraud scheme to reap the $39,000 DRG payments for "COVID plus ventilator".

But ventilators must be managed by experts every hour on the hour or else the air pressure can blow out delicate lung alveoli. Well, due to negligence, that is exactly what was happening. The patients set aside in "hospice" wards were being killed by the ventilators.

---

[111] Gould M. "EXCLUSIVE: 'It's a horror movie.' Nurse working on coronavirus frontline in New York claims the city is 'murdering' COVID-19 patients by putting them on ventilators and causing trauma to the lungs" Daily Mail website. April 27, 2020.

[112] Miller J. "Stricken coronavirus nurse: 'Gross negligence' has patients dying at NYC hospitals" NY Post website. May 5, 2020.

Moreover, most of the ICU patients likely could have been treated with a cocktail of therapies and never have progressed to the critically-ill stage in the first place. But hydroxychloroquine was banned by Governor Cuomo and his Democrat cabal of governors in other states, and remdesivir, steroids, blood thinners, and convalescent plasma were not offered in most cases.

This strategy of dealing with the sickest Wuhan virus patients needlessly killed many thousands of people, one could argue. We will never truly know the number who could have been saved because the medical records have been forged or deleted, according to the whistleblowers.

A White House briefing displayed the deaths by city. The top graph line is New York City, which dwarfs the others.

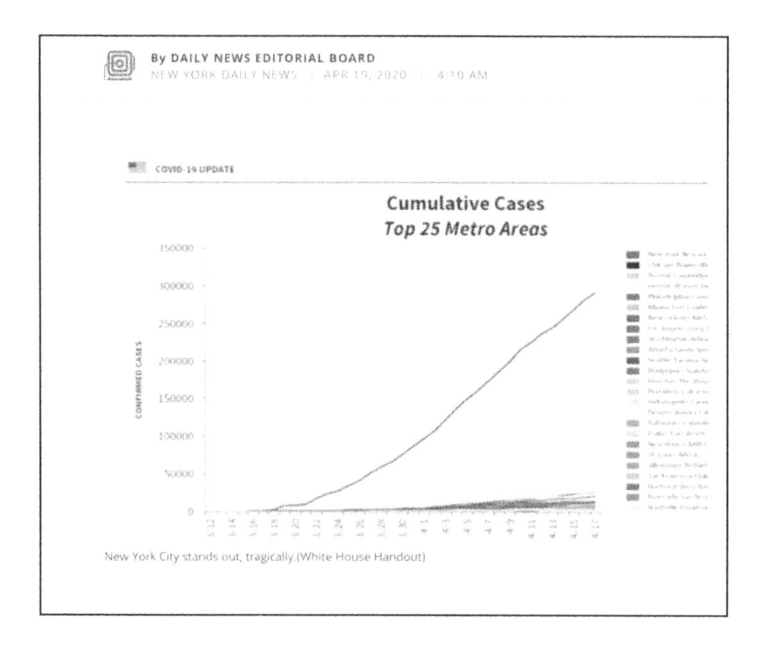

New York City stands out, tragically.(White House Handout)

A mass grave dug by the City of New York in April on remote Hart Island in the middle of Long Island Sound[113]

Clearly, the death toll seen in the New York and New Jersey metropolitan aera was unique to the region. There is no biologically plausible explanation for the differences in deaths between the New York region and the rest of the country. All signs point to human error.

[113] "Coronavirus: New York ramps up mass burials amid outbreak" BBC News website. April 10, 2020

Chapter 8: You Can't Always Get What You Want

On Friday, October 2nd, 2020, the White House announced that President Trump had tested positive for the Wuhan virus. Later in the day, he walked across the lawn onto Marine 1 and headed to Walter Reed Naval National Military Medical Center to be treated with the best possible drugs available on the planet at the time (to be detailed in a subsequent chapter). On Monday, he walked out of Walter Reed, flew back to the White House, and looked to be in 100% health.

How does that treatment strategy and drug regimen compare to what any other American would receive after testing positive? Don't worry about it. What the president received is not meant for you. You can't always get what you want.[114]

The dirty secret that has not been reported (until this book came out) is that medical centers across the nation are still refusing to accept patients with symptoms of the Wuhan virus (as of October, 2020). Even those patients who test positive are told to stay home and drink water, essentially, until their condition deteriorates and they need serious medical care in the ICU. If that sounds like the absolute opposite of what President Trump received, that's because it is.

The medical actions taken after President Trump was diagnosed with the SARS-COV-2 Wuhan virus were correct and cutting edge. The key component of his treatment was the immediate nature of it. We know that this virus has been engineered (i.e. "gain-of-function") in Tony Virus' NIH-funded labs to attack the ACE-2 receptors,

---

[114] President Trump plays this Rolling Stones song at his rallies.

which means blood vessels in our lungs, kidneys, etc. are assaulted, leading to micro-blood-clots. After that, a massive inflammatory cascade is unleashed, which causes more damage. To prevent a serious decline in health, often with permanent affects, the damage must be prevented. This means that the therapies must be given early.

In President Trump's case, he had a medical team willing to see him, draw blood, and perform tests without delay. However, for the rest of us, that type of care is now impossible to obtain from most hospitals.

For the person who is symptomatic, in need of urgent medications, they are literally told to NOT come to emergency room, hospital, or even their primary care doctor's office. They are instructed to make an appointment, in most cases, and drive through some tented parking lot facility to have their nasopharynx swabbed for a PCR test, which takes at least 24-hours to get results. Then, a day or so later, if they are positive, they are still not allowed into a hospital unless they have serious symptoms.

In other words, the current treatment regimens being copied by American hospitals are almost the exact opposite of what should be delivered. The gutless, politically motivated, bureaucrats leading these large quasi-government medical centers, earning multi-million-dollar salaries, are circling the wagons in hope of achieving protection by numbers. They are building the case for the future defense of, "We all did the same thing. Therefore, we all cannot have been committing malpractice on a scale never before seen." But they were. This is a crime against humanity, as will be detailed in subsequent chapters.

I learned of this after my parents came down with symptoms and I tried to have them tested and treated at The Ohio State University Medical Center. I communicated with senior management who informed me of the following protocol: A) People with symptoms, such as cough and fever, are not allowed to be seen in the emergency room. By appointment, they are instructed to drive to an off-campus parking lot to have a nasal-swab PCR test that takes about a day to get back. B) For those who test positive, they are instructed to home-quarantine. No medications, such as hydroxychloroquine, zinc, or vitamin D are prescribed. They are told to stay hydrated. C) Only people in acute respiratory distress, with decreased oxygen saturation (i.e. near death), will be seen by the ER.

To determine whether this was standard procedure or an aberration, I called around. Johns Hopkins, 400-miles to the East, The Cleveland Clinic, 120-miles North, New York University Medical Center, 540-miles to the East, and UCLA, 2,260 miles to the West, all had the same policies of setting up strong defenses around their campuses to keep the sick out.

Why are hospitals preferring these incorrect policies rather than treating the patients urgently? Normally, American medicine would financially reward these hospitals if they gave millions of Americans very costly intravenous medications, such as remdesivir, then costly medical imaging, ICU care, etc. This should be a windfall for them. Why are they missing the opportunity? That is a very good question. The actual answer evades this author, but I have a guess: misguided politics are one reason.

To be clear, lack of medications or personal protective equipment are not the reason hospitals are setting up barriers to treatment. Every drug that President Trump received is available in ample supply to those who need it, with the exception of the still-experimental Regeneron antibody drug. Remdesivir, dexamethasone, hydroxychloroquine (although it appears in this case that Trump did not receive this), vitamins, and even plasma donated form people who have the antibodies, are easily obtained by any large medical center. All of these therapies are effective at saving lives and would generate high profits for the hospitals. So, again the question, why are they not being used on a large scale for regular Americans?

First, one needs to understand that all medical centers are really government institutions, whether they are officially listed as for-profit private hospitals or public hospitals. That is because their revenue is mostly derived from the federal and state governments via Medicare and Medicaid, etc. In many cases, they are the largest employers in the region. They have been turned into jobs creation programs by governors.

So, when this scamdemic first began to be recognized around March of 2020, the Democrat governors called the shots in New York, New Jersey, Connecticut, Pennsylvania, Michigan, California, etc. (Even so-called Republican governors, such a Michael DeWine of Ohio and Greg Abbott of Texas, cowered to the peer pressure and joined the flock of sheep.). Since the epicenter was in New York, that meant Governor Andrew Cuomo was really leading the efforts for much of the nation. As detailed in previous chapters, Cuomo botched it very badly indeed.

However, bad governors and the bureaucracies they run do not like to admit wrongdoing. Their response to mistake is first to deny, then lie, and then double down. As of October, when this chapter was written, nine-months after the first mistakes were made in New York, most hospitals in the country are still doubling down, refusing to admit they were wrong, and still denying crucial early care to people with the Wuhan virus.

Peeling this rotten onion one more layer, what led to Cuomo, *et al*, making these fateful decisions? Well, it was a combination of sheer panic and a desire to avoid bad optics, this author speculates.

In New York, the wealthy regions of the city and state wanted to keep the hot spots in Brooklyn and Queens isolated. Marc Siegel, MD of NYU was on Fox News, via remote feeds from his safe apartment, openly begging sick people to not seek medical care at his hospital. Nicole Saphier, MD, another Fox News contributor, was becoming famous too speaking remotely from her apartment, looking glamorous, never stepping foot in her Memorial Sloan Kettering hospital for months. However, they represented almost all doctors in Manhattan, The Hamptons, wealthy parts of New Jersey, etc. These cowardly doctors were personally afraid of the virus and threw the patients under the bus, in my opinion.

What transpired was an unprecedented act in American modern medicine. In previous pandemics, ranging from the Spanish Flu of 1918 to the Ebola outbreak of 2014, doctors never told the sick to stay away. Bellevue Hospital courageously treated the much deadlier Ebola virus victims, after all.

As the doctors were panicking during this scamdemic, Governor Cuomo was seeing the images from Italian hospitals that were overflowing with patients and wanted to avoid the same bad optics. In fact, the entire strategy from the federal government at the time, led by Tony Virus, was to "flatten the curve" so as to avoid running out of hospital capacity. Therefore, in addition to committing the nursing home massacres detailed previously, Governor Cuomo's New York health officials started to quarantine the actual hospitals from the sick people rather than place the sick people in the hospitals to be quarantined!

This type of backassward, illogical, insane policy by feckless government leaders during times of crises is typical. Many books have been written about it, such as Kurt Vonnegut's Slaughterhouse-Five and Catch-22.

Chapter 9: PCR Testing Does Not Identify Wuhan Virus Infections

As mentioned in the previous chapter, almost all medical centers are still (as of October, 2020) requiring patients with symptoms to first undergo nasal-swab PCR tests. However, those tests require fancy machines at large centralized labs around the country to process. Therefore, they take several days usually to get results.

But that delay is critical. The best way to prevent death and permanent tissue damage from the Wuhan virus is to treat it early, as they did with President Trump.

"Wait", you might ask, "What about those rapid point-of-care tests the White House is touting? And what are antibody tests? Is this all a casedemic?"

It turns out that this entire politically-motivated scamdemic has been driven by the fear created from a casedemic rather than a real pandemic that causes high death rates, such as the Spanish Flu. The tool for this crime against humanity has been the nasal swab PCR test.

First, let's back up and ask, "What is a "pandemic" and who defines it?" It is such a serious classification that it allows for emergency powers of governments to suspend constitutional rights, order lockdowns, and jail people. Democracies can become totalitarian fascist states overnight.

Well, it turns out that in 2009, as the H1N1 Swine Flu outbreak was becoming recognized, the W.H.O. quietly changed the definition of pandemic from that of "An influenza pandemic occurs when a new influenza virus appears against which the human population has no immunity, resulting in several simultaneous epidemics worldwide <u>with enormous numbers of deaths and</u>

illness."[115] to the lower threshold of merely, "An influenza pandemic may occur when a new influenza virus appears against which the human population has no immunity." The phrase "enormous numbers of deaths and illness" had been removed (For a detailed discussion, see the report by Harvard/MIT's Peter Doshi).[116]

This down-classification of pandemic in 2009 led to a massive overreaction by governments to the Swine Flu. It turned out that this virus was not causing enormous numbers of deaths at all.

Of course, as you might have guessed, the humans running the various committees in charge of these definitions were members of the Neuraminidase Inhibitor Susceptibility Network, a group funded by GlaxoSmithKline and Roche.[117] One should always follow the money trail when it comes to large disease-monitoring agencies, such as the W.H.O. or the CDC.

So, when the Wuhan virus began to make the news in January of 2020, The W.H.O. was able to label it as a pandemic and the governments of the world went into fascist totalitarian mode. In the Philippines, people not wearing masks were shot in the head. In Australia and the U.K., people were arrested in their homes. In New York City, orthodox Jews in Brooklyn were literally rounded up by the police in scenes reminiscent of Nazi Germany.

---

[115] Pandemic preparedness [Internet]. Geneva: World Health Organization; 2003 Feb 2. Available from: http://web.archive.org/web/20030202145905/http://www.who.int/csr/disease/influenza/pandemic/en/ [accessed 7 April 2011].

[116] Doshi P. "Bulletin of the World Health Organization 2011" W.H.O. website

[117] Neuraminidase Inhibitor Susceptibility Network. NISN membership [Internet]. 2008. Available from: http://www.nisn.org/au_members.php [accessed 7 April 2011].

But there were not enormous deaths being seen when the Wuhan pandemic was declared. People were not dropping dead by the millions like we saw in the Spanish Flu.

Isolated elderly in nursing homes were mostly succumbing, and we do not even know whether or not they had the actual Wuhan virus or some common flu that is also deadly. The proper tests were not performed (if any testing was done at all before creating bogus death certificates, as detailed in previous chapters).

It turns out that the PCR test for the Wuhan virus that the world has relied on is so unreliable that it is counterproductive, and that is an understatement. The RNA molecular fragments it looks for are not engineered based on the actual Wuhan virus genetics. Then, the way that the test is run makes it far too sensitive and false positives are the normal outcome.[118]

If someone tests positive for the "COVID-19" coronavirus now, it does not mean they have an active viral infection. What the test result likely means is that it was a false positive, either because the patient had traces of some other "common cold" coronavirus or inactive fragment of old RNA that do not represent functioning virus.

---

[118] The make and model of the PCR test is the Applied Biosystems 7500 Fast Dx Real-Time PCR System with SDS version 1.4 software."

From a July, 2020 CDC technical manual on the use and interpretation of the PCR test, it states:

> "- Detection of viral RNA may not indicate the presence of infectious virus or that 2019-nCoV is the causative agent for clinical symptoms.
>
> - The performance of this test has not been established for monitoring treatment of 2019-nCoV infection.
>
> - The performance of this test has not been established for screening of blood or blood products for the presence of 2019-nCoV.
>
> - This test cannot rule out diseases caused by other bacterial or viral pathogens."[119]

International class-action lawyer Reiner Fuellmich issued a lengthy oral statement on this and other matters in a video called Crimes Against Humanity. From the transcript of that video:[120]

"It is still not clear whether there has ever been a scientifically correct isolation of the Wuhan virus, so that nobody knows exactly what we are looking for when we test, especially since this virus, just like the flu viruses,

[119] "CDC 2019-Novel Coronavirus (2019-nCoV) Real-Time RT-PCR Diagnostic Panel" FDA website. July 13, 2020

[120] Fuellmich R. "Crimes Against Humanity" YouTube. https://youtu.be/kr04gHbP5MQ October 3, 2020

mutates quickly. The PCR swabs take one or two sequences of a molecule that are invisible to the human eye and therefore need to be amplified in many cycles to make it visible. **Everything over 35 cycles is - as reported by the New York Times and others - considered completely unreliable and scientifically unjustifiable.** However, the Drosten test, as well as the WHO-recommended tests that followed his example, are set to 45 cycles. Can that be because of the desire to produce as many positive results as possible and thereby provide the basis for the false assumption that a large number of infections have been detected?

The test cannot distinguish inactive and reproductive matter. That means that a positive result may happen because the test detects e.g. a piece of debris, a fragment of a molecule, which may signal nothing else than that the immune system of the person tested won a battle with the common cold in the past.

Even Drosten himself declared in an interview with a German business magazine in 2014, at that time concerning the alleged detection of an infection with the MERS virus, allegedly with the help of the PCR test, that these PCR tests are so highly sensitive that even very healthy and non-infectious people may test positive. At that time, he also became very much aware of the powerful role of the panic and fear-mongering media, as you'll see at the end of the following quote.

He said: "If, for example, such a pathogen scurries over the nasal mucosa of a nurse for a day or so without her getting sick or noticing anything else, then she is suddenly a MERS case. This could also explain the explosion of case numbers in Saudi Arabia. In addition, the media there have made this into an incredible sensation".

Has he forgotten this, or is he deliberately concealing this in the Corona context, because Corona is a very lucrative business opportunity for the pharmaceutical industry as a whole and for Mr. Olfert Landt, his co-author in many studies and also: a PCR test producer? In my view, it is completely implausible that he forgot in 2020 what he knew about the PCR tests and told a business magazine in 2014.

In short: This test cannot detect any infection, contrary to all false claims stating that it can. An infection, a so-called "hot infection", requires that the virus, or rather: a fragment of a molecule which may be a virus - is not just found somewhere, e.g. in the throat of a person without causing any damage (that would be a cold infection). Rather, a hot infection requires that the virus penetrates into the cells, replicates there and causes symptoms such as headaches, or a sore throat. Only then is a person really infected in the sense of a hot infection, because only then is a person contagious, that is: able to infect others. Until then, it is completely harmless for both the host and all other people that the host comes into contact with.

Once again: This means that positive test results - contrary to all other claims, e.g. by Drosten, Wieler or the WHO – mean nothing with respect to infections, as even the CDC knows as quoted above. **Meanwhile, a number of highly respected scientists worldwide assume that there has never been a corona pandemic, but only a PCR test pandemic."**

So, the PCR tests being used by the world are looking for RNA sequences that do not narrowly define the Wuhan virus with specificity, but instead catch in a broad net the RNA from related common-cold viruses or contaminants. The false positive rate is 90% or more according to some reports.[121] It is worse than merely unreliable, it is misleading.

The false PCR positive tests do not mean anyone is ill with an active infection. However, the global media and governments interpret them as if the tests results are somehow surrogates for the missing deaths that one should see during a scary pandemic. This is not a true pandemic with "enormous numbers of deaths and illness".

This is a politically motivated scamdemic driven by a casedemic fueled by bogus PCR tests, and there is no end in sight. Given the high false positive rates, people will be told they have the "COVID-19" for years and years if this insanity is not stopped.

Already, political hack Tony Virus is fearmongering that social distancing will be needed for years (unless it relates to himself attending a baseball game doing neither). During a rogue media interview, he stated in classic Fuacian doom-speak that life would not be back to normal for years, even if the vaccines are effective.[122]

Are there any better ways to test for the Wuhan virus? There are and they will be discussed next.

---

[121] Yeadon M. "Lies, Damned Lies and Health Statistics – the Deadly Danger of False Positives" Lockdown Skeptics website. September 20, 2020.

[122] Kubota S. "Fauci warns COVID-19 vaccine won't end social distancing, public health measures" Today Show website. September 25, 2020.

Chapter 10: The Proper Protocols for Testing and Treatment of the Wuhan Virus

In the previous chapters, I have detailed how almost all of the hospitals in the nation, and likely the world, have treated patients with the Wuhan virus in almost the exact opposite manner in which they should have been treated. Due to cowardice and politics, the hospitals have quarantined themselves like medieval fortresses under siege by an invisible enemy carried on the barbarians (otherwise known as sick people in need of care).

As a result, almost every major medical center is now bleeding cash and laying off employees. The populations they serve have been deprived not only of treatment for the Wuhan virus, but also less urgent care.

Yet the CEO's of these institutions are patting themselves on their collective backs as if they have handled this properly. They still collect their multi-million-dollar paychecks.

What should happen going forward in treatment protocols? Will the dramatically different care that The President of the United States received shame these institutions into changing? Will Alex Azar, The United States Secretary of Health and Human Services, which is in charge of Medicare and Medicaid, the FDA, CMS, etc., sit back and watch this crime against humanity unfold?

This is what I think should be the proper protocols for treatment during this scamdemic. It is very similar to the care that president Trump received. I sent this proposal to Secretary Azar and several leaders of major medical centers:

Screening and Triage

- No patient should be told by any hospital operator or automated phone-tree message to stay home and do nothing. Just like any other illness, patients should be encouraged to seek immediate care.

- Just as hospitals have done now, special outdoor tented clinics should be established for testing, but no appointment should be required.

- The virus test performed at these special triage centers should be rapid point-of-care tests that are not based on PCR technology. These are many times less likely than PCR to generate false positives. Only people actively sick typically trigger positives from these point-of-care tests.

- In addition, a pulse oximeter measurement and temperature measurement should be taken.

This simple triage strategy would immediately stop the casedemic driving the scamdemic, that has caused untold morbidity and mortality from the lockdowns. Patients would receive immediate news and relief, if they are negative, or care if they are positive.

SARS-COV-2-positive patients with serious symptoms

- For test-positive SARS-COV-2 symptomatic patients of any age should be admitted to the hospital and given IV remdesivir, zinc, Vitamin D, and any other newly approved drug that becomes available, such as the Regeneron antibody cocktail given to President Trump.

- However, their test status should first be verified by in-house viral load tests that require blood draws, if possible. If these tests cannot be performed within hours, then the patent should be treated based on the assumption they are positive given the rapid tests.

- The decisions of when or if to use supplemental oxygen, antibiotics, blood thinners, or dexamethasone should be made on a case-by-case basis.

- Notably, chest CT-scans should be avoided. They impart cancer-causing levels of radiation and are entirely unnecessary to boot.

- Likewise, ventilators should be avoided at all costs. Oxygen masks suffice.

SARS-COV-2-positive patients with mild symptoms

- For test-positive patients with mild symptoms (i.e. no fever and good O2 saturation) and no risk factors (i.e. under the age of 70 and no diabetes or serious kidney, liver, lung, or immune system ailments), they can be treated in the outpatient setting.

- Before being sent home from the triage center, however, blood should be drawn for proper verification of the Wuhan virus status. Then, they should be given prescriptions for hydroxychloroquine, Vitamin D and zinc, and a pulse oximeter machine. Ideally, a pharmacy would be set up inside the triage center.

- Then, using telemedicine, doctors should monitor the oxygen and temperature. If it worsens, they should be admitted to the hospital.

For regular flu patients

- It should be noted that many people in the triage centers will turn out to have the regular flu. They should be given Tamiflu if mildly symptomatic, then monitored via telemedicine. Patients with severe respiratory decompensation should be admitted.

For immobile nursing home patients

- For patients immobile and unable to drive to a triage center, likely in an assisted living center, they are also the most vulnerable to death from the Wuhan virus or flu.

- Teams of traveling doctors should be assembled. Ideally, the doctors and nurses should be antibody-positive and, therefore, far less likely to transmit dangerous infections to the people they treat (i.e. they are immune after recovering from a past infection).[123]

- Proper antibody testing is achieved only by administering six different assays for three different forms of antibodies, per the Icelandic study.[124]

If these "Greer protocols" became the new gold standard, I bet you a lot of money that the already-low death rates would approach zero. Nobody, not even the 90-year-old nursing home patient, should die from the Wuhan virus.

---

[123] Iyer A. et al. "Persistence and decay of human antibody responses to the receptor binding domain of SARS-CoV-2 spike protein in COVID-19 patients" Science Immunology. October 8, 2020:
Vol. 5, Issue 52

[124] D.F. Gudbjartsson, et al. "Humoral Immune Response to SARS-CoV-2 in Iceland" NEJM online release September 7, 2020

Chapter 11: The Great Maskquerade

The following claim will sound so unbelievable as to make me seem crazy, but it is true, and I can prove it. I was the first person in media or medicine to recommend wearing masks to protect against the Wuhan virus.

On March 9th, 2020, I stepped into the Lower Manhattan studio of John Tabacco's on Broadway where he filmed his Liquid Lunch show, produced by Frank Morano (the lockdowns eventually closed down his operations).[125] He asked me how one could protect against the virus and I explained that masks might help in certain situations. I explained that masks mostly helped protect people against the bad habit of touching one's mouth and eyes. That is how viruses are spread from person to person, more so than by breathing aerosolized droplets.

Almost no one was wearing a mask at the time and the lockdowns had not yet begun. But fear was in the air. Hand-cleanser gels were the main weapon against infection. Subway usage was down. It was the eve of the Great Scamdemic.

At the time, our government officials were telling us that masks were silly. Tony Virus, the Surgeon General Jerome Adams, and the official stance of the CDC were all strongly opposed to the mass use by the public of wearing masks. I knew that they were lying to us in order to prevent a run on supply of masks that hospital workers needed and I said so on that little TV program.

However, never in my wildest dreams did I imagine that mask mandates would become the abused symbol of

---

[125] Greer SE. "BizTV's Liquid Lunch interviews Steven E. Greer, MD about the pandemic" GreerJournal.com March 9, 2020

obedience for the Marxists who quickly used fearmongering to close down the U.S. economy in hopes of derailing President Trump's re-election bid.

Broad-stroke, one-size-fits-all, government mandates to wear masks do more harm than good. Many people have poor lung function from COPD, asthma, or other ailments. The masks increase the CO2 concentration they inhale and lower their O2 blood saturation levels. Reused masks also spread bacterial diseases.

Only in proper settings can masks possibly be of any use, and even then, the data are weak. For example, surgical teams wear masks in the operating room to prevent our oral droplets from entering an open surgical site. But the fact is that our low-tech masks do not prevent this from happening.[126,127] If a surgeon is really serious about preventing infection, they wear space suits with separate air supplies, as one sees in orthopedic surgery.

Other appropriate uses of masks are during visits with nursing home patients, cancer patients with compromised immune systems, or other similar settings. However, again, the data are lacking.

As recently as October, 2019, the W.H.O. issued a report that reviewed the various studies on masks, handwashing, and social distancing, which concluded,

---

[126] Ha'eri GB, et al. "The efficacy of standard surgical face masks: an investigation using "tracer particles" Clinical Orthopaedics and Related Research, 30 Apr 1980, (148):160-162

[127] Fetzer J. "Studies of Surgical Masks Efficacy: Masks are useless in preventing the spread of disease (even during surgery)" JamesFetzer.org website August 14, 2020

"no evidence that face masks are effective in reducing transmission of laboratory-confirmed influenza"[128]

The executive summary states:

"Here, we systematically review and evaluate the evidence base on the effectiveness and impact of community mitigation measures for pandemic and interpandemic influenza. This evidence base will contribute to updated public health guidelines for community mitigation measures for influenza. The scope of this review includes evidence on the effectiveness of interventions such as personal protective measures, environmental measures, social distancing measures, and travel-related measures. Consideration is also given to the feasibility of each intervention, including potential ethical issues.

We found that there is a limited evidence base on the effectiveness of non-pharmaceutical community mitigation measures. There are a number of high-quality randomized controlled trials demonstrating that personal measures (e.g. hand hygiene and face masks) have at best a small effect on transmission, with the caveat that higher compliance in a severe pandemic might improve efficacy.

But there are few randomized trials for other NPIs, and much of the evidence base is from observational studies and computer simulations. School closures can reduce transmission, but would need to be carefully timed to achieve mitigation objectives, while there may be ethical issues to consider. Travel-related measures are unlikely to

---

[128] The World Health organization. "Non-pharmaceutical public health measures for mitigating the risk and impact of epidemic and pandemic influenza" W.H.O. website. October 2019.

be successful in most locations because current screening tools such as thermal scanners cannot identify presymptomatic and asymptomatic infections, and travel restrictions and travel bans are likely to have prohibitive economic consequences."

Then, the W.H.O. reversed course in June of 2020, once the scamdemic had become a political tool, and issued guidance recommending the wearing of masks to protect against the Wuhan virus. However, because we live in a world where people read only the headlines from propaganda outlets that grossly misinterpret "science", few bothered to read this actual report. If one does read the report, they will find that the W.H.O. again states there is no evidence to support the use of masks by entire populations of healthy people as a means of prophylaxis!

"There are currently no studies that have evaluated the effectiveness and potential adverse effects of universal or targeted continuous mask use by health workers in preventing transmission of SARS-CoV-2. Despite the lack of evidence the great majority of the WHO COVID-19 IPC GDG members supports the practice of health workers and caregivers in clinical areas (irrespective of whether there are COVID-19 or other patients in the clinical areas) in geographic settings where there is known or suspected community transmission of COVID-19, to continuously wear a medical mask throughout their shift, apart from when eating and drinking or changing the mask after caring for a patient requiring droplet/contact precautions for other reasons (e.g., influenza), to avoid any possibility of cross-transmission…

Studies of influenza, influenza-like illness, and human coronaviruses (not including COVID-19) provide evidence that the use of a medical mask can prevent the spread of infectious droplets from a symptomatic infected person (source control) to someone else and potential contamination of the environment by these droplets. **There is limited evidence that wearing a medical mask by healthy individuals in households, in particular those who share a house with a sick person, or among attendees of mass gatherings may be beneficial as a measure preventing transmission**. A recent meta-analysis of these observational studies, with the intrinsic biases of observational data, showed that either disposable surgical masks or reusable 12–16-layer cotton masks were associated with protection of healthy individuals within households and among contacts of cases.

This could be considered to be indirect evidence for the use of masks (medical or other) by healthy individuals in the wider community; however, these studies suggest that such individuals would need to be in close proximity to an infected person in a household or at a mass gathering where physical distancing cannot be achieved, to become infected with the virus.

Results from cluster randomized controlled trials on the use of masks among young adults living in university residences in the United States of America indicate that face masks may reduce the rate of influenza-like illness, but showed no impact on risk of laboratory-confirmed influenza.

At present, there is no direct evidence (from studies on COVID-19 and in

healthy people in the community) on the effectiveness of universal masking of healthy people in the community to prevent infection with respiratory viruses, including COVID-19."[129]

Those quotes are not from some old irrelevant article made obsolete by "new science". They come from a W.H.O. report issued in June of 2020, long after the lockdowns and mask mandates had hurled the world into a state of totalitarianism!

OK, so the W.H.O. is not a credible scientific organization, one might say. What have the hard-core scientific journals reported on the matter?

The New England Journal of Medicine posted a paper in May of 2020 concluding that masks for the masses was a complete waste of time. This is not aging very well:

"**What is clear, however, is that universal masking alone is not a panacea. A mask will not protect providers caring for a patient with active Covid-19** if it's not accompanied by meticulous hand hygiene, eye protection, gloves, and a gown. A mask alone will not prevent health care workers with early Covid-19 from contaminating their hands and spreading the virus to

---

[129] The World Health Organization. "Advice on the use of masks in the context of COVID-19" W.H.O. website. June, 2020.

patients and colleagues. Focusing on universal masking alone may, paradoxically, lead to more transmission of Covid-19 if it diverts attention from implementing more fundamental infection control measures…

It is also clear that masks serve symbolic roles. **Masks are not only tools, they are also talismans that may help increase health care workers' perceived sense of safety**, well-being, and trust in their hospitals."[130]

The CDC issued a report in September of 2020 that revealed 92% of all people testing positive for the virus wore masks.[131]

Morbidity and Mortality Weekly Report

TABLE. (*Continued*) Characteristics of symptomatic adults ≥18 years who were outpatients in 11 academic health c positive and negative SARS-CoV-2 test results (N = 314)* — United States, July 1–29, 2020

	No. (%)	
Characteristic	Case-patients (n = 154)	Control participants (n = 160)
Previous close contact with a person with known COVID-19 (missing = 1)		
No	89 (57.8)	136 (85.5)
Yes	65 (42.2)	23 (14.5)
Relationship to close contact with known COVID-19 (n = 88)		
Family	33 (50.8)	5 (21.7)
Friend	9 (13.8)	4 (17.4)
Work colleague	11 (16.9)	6 (26.1)
Other**	6 (9.2)	8 (34.8)
Multiple	6 (9.2)	0 (0.0)
Reported use of cloth face covering or mask 14 days before illness onset (missing = 2)		
Never	6 (3.9)	5 (3.1)
Rarely	6 (3.9)	6 (3.8)
Sometimes	11 (7.2)	7 (4.4)
Often	22 (14.4)	23 (14.5)
Always	108 (70.6)	118 (74.2)

---

[130] Klompas M. "Universal Masking in Hospitals in the Covid-19 Era" NEJM website. May 21, 2020

[131] "Morbidity and Mortality Weekly Report" CDC website. September 11, 2020

The only randomized clinical trial to study whether or not cloth masks reduce the chances of contracting respiratory virial illnesses also concluded that masks do not work. In fact, they are harmful:

> "Conclusions: This study is the first RCT of cloth masks, and the results caution against the use of cloth masks. This is an important finding to inform occupational health and safety. Moisture retention, reuse of cloth masks and poor filtration may result in increased risk of infection. Further research is needed to inform the widespread use of cloth masks globally. However, as a precautionary measure, cloth masks should not be recommended for HCWs, particularly in high-risk situations, and guidelines need to be updated." [132]

A world renowned neurologist from Germany, Margarite Griesz-Brisson MD, PhD, also weighed in explaining how masks can be harmful to the brain:

"The reinhalation of our exhaled air will without a doubt create oxygen deficiency and a flooding of carbon dioxide. We know that **the human brain is very sensitive to oxygen deprivation**. There are nerve cells for example in the hippocampus that can't be longer than 3 minutes without oxygen - they cannot survive.

[132] MacIntyre CR, Seale H, Dung TC, et al. "A cluster randomised trial of cloth masks compared with medical masks in healthcare workers BMJ website. April 22, 2015

I do not wear a mask, I need my brain to think. I want to have a clear head when I deal with my patients, and not be in a carbon dioxide-induced anaesthesia.

There is no unfounded medical exemption from face masks because **oxygen deprivation is dangerous for every single brain**. It must be the free decision of every human being whether they want to wear a mask that is absolutely ineffective to protect themselves from a virus.

For children and adolescents, masks are an absolute no-no. Children and adolescents have an extremely active and adaptive immune system and they need a constant interaction with the microbiome of the Earth. Their brain is also incredibly active, as it is has so much to learn. The child's brain, or the youth's brain, is thirsting for oxygen. The more metabolically active the organ is, the more oxygen it requires. In children and adolescents every organ is metabolically active.[133]

So, where did Tony Virus weigh in on this crucial debate? As the outbreak began to unfold, before it was being politicized, Tony is memorialized on video stating several times that masks are silly and should be discouraged from use by the peasant masses.

In one pre-scamdemic TV interview, Tony said,

> "When you are in the middle of an outbreak, wearing a mask might make people feel a little bit better (with finger air-quotes), and it

---

[133] Maria, H. "German Neurologist Warns Against Wearing Facemasks: 'Oxygen Deprivation Causes Permanent Neurological Damage'" Scott.net. October 6, 2020

> might even block a droplet, but it's not providing the perfect protection that people think that it is. And often, there are unintended consequences, because people keep fiddling with the mask and they keep touching their face."[134]

During another Fuacian rogue interview, he told Spectrum News,

> "There is no reason for anyone, right now in the United States, with regard to coronavirus, to wear a mask....There's this misperception that wearing a mask, even if you were in an area where there was transmission, is going to absolutely protect you. A mask is more appropriate for someone who is infected, to prevent them from infecting you."[135]

Later, Tony Virus admitted to congress that he was lying all along out of concern that healthcare workers would run out of masks of the entire population demanded them. In June, Rep. David McKinley (R) asked whether he regretted recommending against masks as recently as March 31st. An angry Tony Virus replied,

> "OK. We're going to play that game...I don't regret that (i.e. lying to the American public) because,...at that time, there was a paucity of equipment (i.e. masks) that our healthcare providers needed...We did not

---

[134] YouTube. unknown origin. https://youtu.be/zyisVNez4Ms
[135] YouTube. Spectrum News. https://youtu.be/9XqXXyAMn3k

want to divert masks and PPE away from them…"[136]

But Tony Virus was never elected by any American to any job. He is a career Deep State bureaucrat, not the omnipotent wise Gandalf of the nation. Where did he get the idea that it was his job to lie, degrading the trust in science, just to protect us?

By the time Fall, 2020 came around, before the important election, Tony Virus had not only done a 180 and become a mask advocate, but he was doomsaying that the scamdemic would not end for years. People would be forced to social distance and wear masks for years, as previously detailed.

Somebody in high levels of the federal government, with the proven unreliable track record of Tony Virus, should be fired under normal circumstances. When their mistake, or lies, lead to crimes against humanity, they should be prosecuted, as will be detailed in subsequent chapters.

The entire campaign to have everyone on the planet wear masks is a maskquerade. As the NEJM authors stated, masks began as voodoo talismans, or gimmicks to make us think we were doing something to protect against the invisible enemy. Then, they morphed into Nazi-like passport papers, visible proof of obeyance to the Marxists driving the fascist totalitarian state power granted to them by pandemic laws. A bare face without a mask became a scarlet letter of shame.

---

[136] CNN. YouTube. https://www.youtube.com/watch?v=Sqex07kJhzU June 23, 2020

Chapter 12: Lockdowns Do Not Work

The abuse of mask mandates described in the previous chapter is part of the bigger crime against humanity caused by irrational government edicts to "socially distance" so as to "flatten the curve", which became what is now known as "lockdowns". But make no mistake, a lockdown is simply a euphemism for totalitarian government house-arrest orders and the suspension of civil liberties.

The lockdowns have been illegal and unjustified. There is no evidence that they have saved any lives. In fact, the opposite is true. There is strong evidence that they have caused untold numbers of deaths, as will be explained.

No other person in the world shares more blame for the lockdowns than Anthony Fauci. As detailed in Chapter 2, it all started on March 11, 2020 when Tony Virus spoke before a congressional hearing and cautioned against sporting events with fans in arenas. From thereon, having tasted the sweet nectar of power, he urged for the lockdowns, all in the name of "flattening the curve" to prevent the hospitals from being overburdened.

A lockdown is an umbrella term that encompasses the closure of "non-essential business", mask mandates, the banning of crowds, and special police forces assigned to "contact tracing" (i.e. people who visit personal homes of anyone thought to be out of line and arrests them). All of those actions have caused the U.S. GDP to implode 33% in the second quarter of 2020, which has never been seen before.[137]

---

[137] Horsely S. "3 Months Of Hell: U.S. Economy Drops 32.9% In Worst GDP Report Ever" NPR website. July 30, 2020

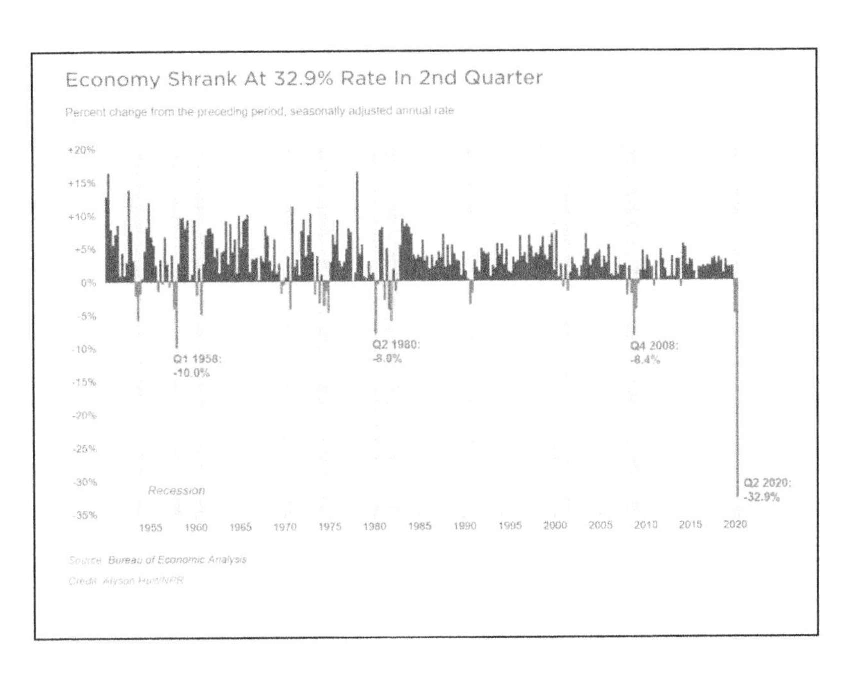
Economy Shrank At 32.9% Rate In 2nd Quarter
Percent change from the preceding period, seasonally adjusted annual rate
+20%
+15%
+10%
+5%
0%
-5%
-10%
-15%
-20%
-25%
-30%
-35%
Q1 1958:
-10.0%
Q2 1980:
-8.0%
Q4 2008:
-8.4%
Q2 2020:
-32.9%
Recession
1955 1960 1965 1970 1975 1980 1985 1990 1995 2000 2005 2010 2015 2020
Source: Bureau of Economic Analysis
Credit: Alyson Hurt/NPR

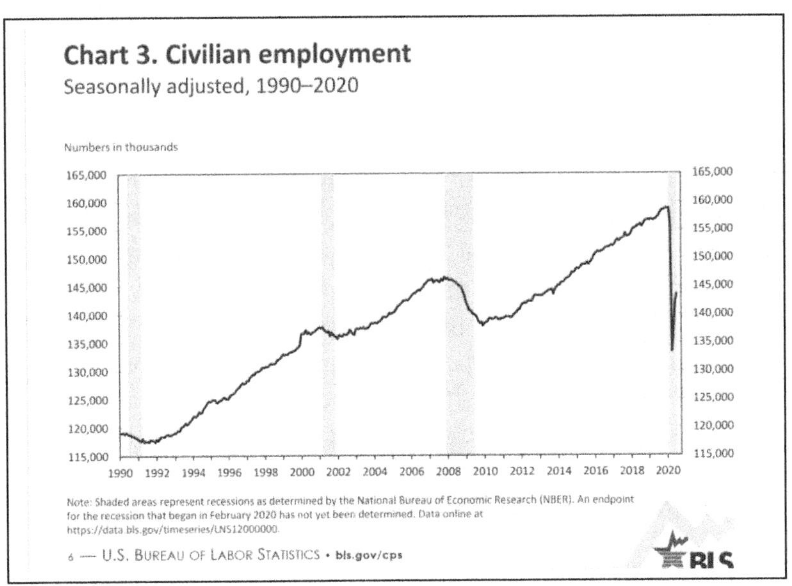
Chart 3. Civilian employment
Seasonally adjusted, 1990–2020
Numbers in thousands
165,000
160,000
155,000
150,000
145,000
140,000
135,000
130,000
125,000
120,000
115,000
1990 1992 1994 1996 1998 2000 2002 2004 2006 2008 2010 2012 2014 2016 2018 2020
Note: Shaded areas represent recessions as determined by the National Bureau of Economic Research (NBER). An endpoint for the recession that began in February 2020 has not yet been determined. Data online at https://data.bls.gov/timeseries/LNS12000000.
6 — U.S. Bureau of Labor Statistics • bls.gov/cps
BLS

The blow to the economy led to a staggering loss of 30 million jobs. To put it in perspective, that is five to ten-times greater than seen in any other recession before (shaded vertical bands in the graph above).

When a huge portion of the population suddenly becomes unemployed, and then is told to stay indoors and not socialize, the impact on health is devastating.

.The CDC reported:

"Elevated levels of adverse mental health conditions, substance use, and suicidal ideation were reported by adults in the United States in June 2020. The prevalence of symptoms of anxiety disorder was approximately three times those reported in the second quarter of 2019 (25.5% versus 8.1%), and **prevalence of depressive disorder was approximately four times that reported in the second quarter of 2019** (24.3% versus 6.5%)

Mental health conditions are disproportionately affecting specific populations, especially young adults, Hispanic persons, black persons, essential workers, unpaid caregivers for adults, and those receiving treatment for preexisting psychiatric conditions. Unpaid caregivers for adults, many of whom are currently providing critical aid to persons at increased risk for severe illness from COVID-19, had a higher incidence of adverse mental and behavioral health conditions compared with others. Although unpaid caregivers of children were not evaluated in this study, approximately 39% of unpaid caregivers for adults shared a household with children (compared with 27% of other respondents). Caregiver workload, especially in multigenerational caregivers, should be considered for future assessment of mental health, given the findings of this report and hardships potentially faced by caregivers."[138]

Making matters worse, the entire healthcare system was almost shut down as well. As detailed in Chapter 10, the cowardly sheep in charge of the medical centers flocked together and began to quarantine the hospitals from the patients. Not only were people with the virus told to stay away, but most "elective procedures" were cancelled too. However, those were not so "elective".

Because people have stopped getting routine screenings for colorectal and breast cancers, those tumor types alone are expected to cause tens of thousands of increases in deaths over the next decade.

"In general, the earlier one receives cancer treatment, the better the results. There already has been a steep drop in cancer diagnoses in the United States since the start of the pandemic, but there is no reason to believe the actual incidence of cancer has dropped. Cancers being missed now will still come to light eventually, but at a later stage ("upstaging") and with worse prognoses. At many hospitals, so-called "elective" cancer treatments and surgeries have been deprioritized to preserve clinical capacity for COVID-19 patients. For example, some patients are receiving less intense chemotherapy and/or radiotherapy, and in other cases, patients' operations to remove a newly detected tumor are being delayed. There can be no doubt that the COVID-19 pandemic is causing

[138] Czeisler M. "Mental Health, Substance Use, and Suicidal Ideation During the COVID-19 Pandemic — United States, June 24–30, 2020" *Weekly* / August 14, 2020 / 69(32);1049–1057

delayed diagnosis and suboptimal care for people with cancer.

What will be the likely impact of the pandemic on cancer mortality in the United States? Modeling the effect of COVID-19 on cancer screening and treatment for breast and colorectal cancer (which together account for about one-sixth of all cancer deaths) over the next decade suggests almost 10,000 excess deaths from breast and colorectal cancer deaths; that is, a ~1% increase in deaths from these tumor types during a period when we would expect to see almost 1,000,000 deaths from these two diseases types. The number of excess deaths per year would peak in the next year or two. This analysis is conservative, as it does not consider other cancer types, it does not account for the additional nonlethal morbidity from upstaging, and it assumes a moderate disruption in care that completely resolves after 6 months. It also does not account for regional variations in the response to the pandemic, and these effects may be less severe in parts of the country with shorter or less severe lockdowns."[139]

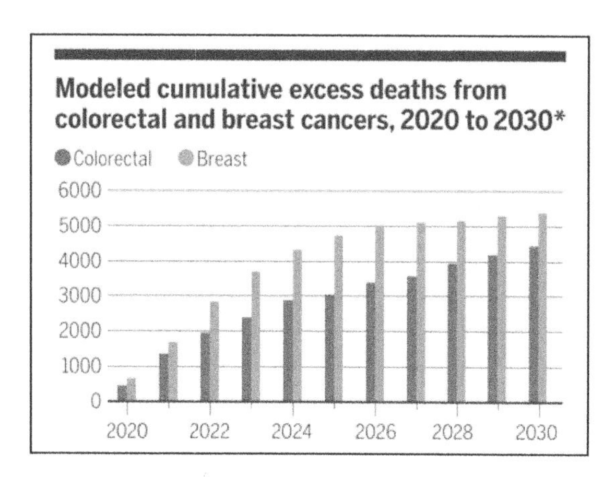

[139] Sharpless N. "COVID-19 and cancer" Science website. 19 Jun 2020: Vol. 368, Issue 6497, pp. 1290

In October of 2020, the CDC issued a report[140] showing the excess deaths (i.e. the actual number of deaths compared to what was forecasted based on past years) and there was already a spike in mortality seen, likely caused by lockdowns. In the graph below is shown the number of deaths after those caused by the Wuhan virus were subtracted. The most likely explanation for the increases are that the entire medical system was almost closed down for more than six-months, and senior citizens isolated in solitary confinement in nursing homes died from the consequences of the dementia that isolation brings on.

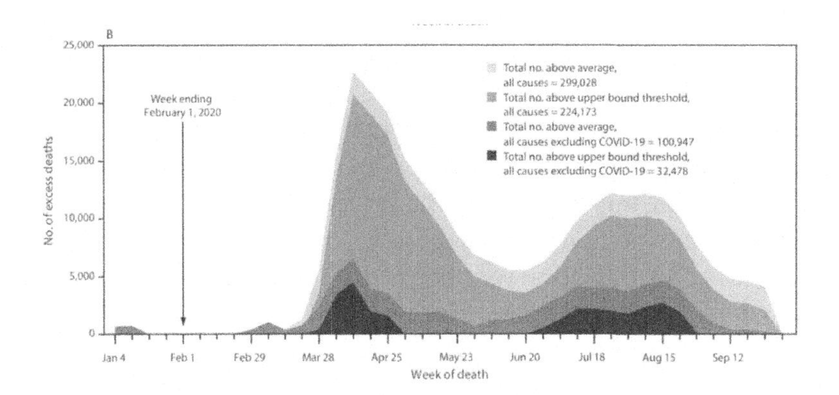

[140] Rossen L, et al. "Excess Deaths Associated with COVID-19, by Age and Race and Ethnicity — United States, January 26–October 3, 2020" Morbidity and Mortality Weekly Report (*MMWR*). CDC website. October 20, 2020

Way to go, Tony Virus and the Marxists now running the Democrat party to which you pander. Are you all proud of yourselves? You committed these crimes against humanity in a vain attempt for political power.

Were these economic and health catastrophes unavoidable? Were the lockdowns essential in order to prevent tens of millions of deaths from the Wuhan virus? You know the answer.

In every country where lockdowns were ordered, the death rates and numbers of Wuhan virus cases increased. This is because it is impossible to enforce true lockdowns and masks do not work to prevent the spread of a respiratory virus.

Also, lockdowns merely delay the inevitable. A viral communicable disease does not go away until herd immunity is reached.

In a nutshell, herd immunity is when a critical mass of the population develops antibodies to a virus making it harder for the virus to jump from one person to another. This is how all outbreaks come to an end. Vaccines are one way to create antibodies, but the far more common way is for people to actually contract the virus (viral outbreaks also dissipate when the weather warms and the virus mutates into a less virulent form.)

Apologies, but another "I said it first" boastful moment is in order. This author was the first person in the media to proclaim that the world had likely reached herd immunity status, in an essay[141] and then on New York's WABC radio with Frank Morano. [142] A few days later, Frank interviewed Senator Rand Paul, MD and they

---

[141] Greer SE. "Exclusive: The human population has already reached the herd immunity state for The Wuhan virus" GreerJournal.com. July 23, 2020. (Also, see "Essays" section at the end of this book)

[142] Greer SE, Morano F. "WLIR's Frank Morano interviews Steven E. Greer, MD about The Wuhan virus and herd immunity: 7-23-2020" GreerJournal.com. July 23, 2020

discussed herd immunity.[143] A few days after that, the new White House pandemic expert, Scott Atlas, MD, took up the cause of herd immunity, and the rest is history as the Democrat party instructed its media outlets to smear Dr. Atlas for daring to suggest that the scamdemic was over.

Sweden is the best clinical trial of lockdowns. Swedes were the only ones to defy the nation-shaming peer pressure to close businesses and mandate masks. They carried on with their lives as normal. Rather than seeing large increases in excess deaths, they saw no changes at all. The Swedish hospitals were not overflowing. School children and teachers were not dying.

In a politically-left-biased article in *Science*, even it admits that the excess deaths in Sweden were far less than nearby England where strict lockdowns were enforced by the punishment of arrest (see graph below). The author spins the data as evidence that Sweden's decision to not enact lockdowns came at the high price of death,

---

"Another way to measure the pandemic's impact is to look at "excess deaths," the difference between the number of people who died this year and average deaths in earlier years. Those curves show Sweden did not suffer as many excess deaths as England and Wales—whose tolls were among Europe's highest—but many more than Germany and its Nordic neighbors (see graphic, p. 161). Immigrant communities were hit very hard. Between March and September, 111 people from Somalia and 247 from Syria died, compared with 5-year averages of 34 and 93, respectively.

[143] Greer SE, Morano F. "WLIR's Frank Morano interviews Steven E. Greer, MD about The Wuhan virus and herd immunity: 8-3-2020" GreerJournal.com. August 3, 2020

And the virus took a shocking toll on the most vulnerable. It had free rein in nursing homes, where nearly 1000 people died in a matter of weeks. Stockholm's nursing homes ended up losing 7% of their 14,000 residents to the virus. The vast majority were not taken to hospitals." [144]

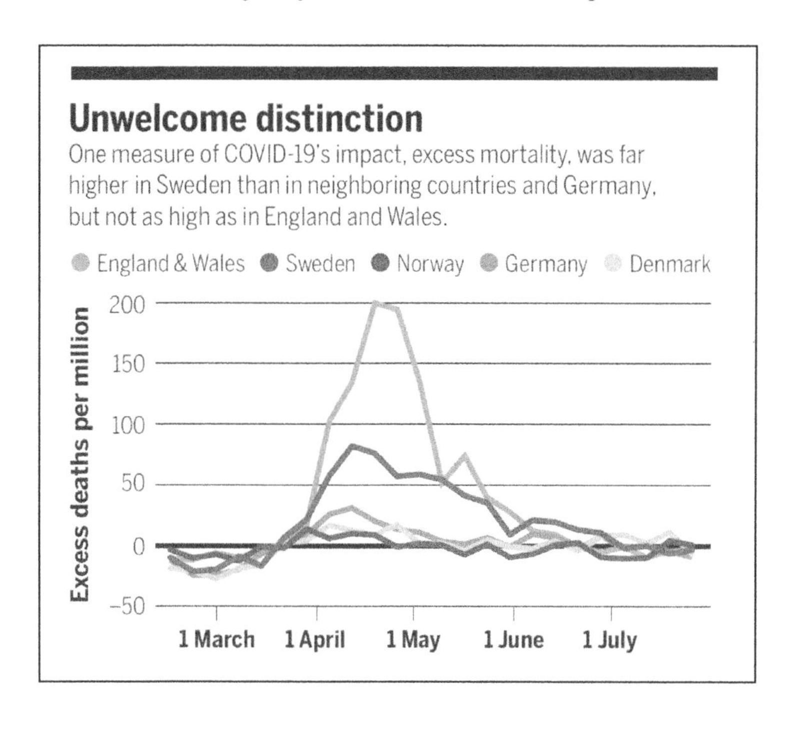

But those comments actually explain how Sweden's overall population was NOT killed at an excessive rate. The entire spike in the death curve was caused by nursing homes and immigrant neighborhoods. However, Sweden has more people from those subgroups than Finland or Norway do. Moreover, changes in nursing home policies

[144] Vogel G. "Sweden's gamble" Science website. Oct 9, 2020, Vol. 370, Issue 6513, pp. 159-163

eventually resulted in lower death rates, the article goes on to state.

The article makes no effort to explain the increases in deaths caused by lockdowns, as detailed previously in this chapter. In England, where lockdowns were severe, what was causing the excess death rate? Was it caused by alcoholism, suicide, or worsening dementia in nursing homes due to isolation?

What about other parts of the world? Did lockdowns work there? The American Institute of Economic Research analyzed this and found that draconian lockdowns did not prevent deaths from the Wuhan virus.[145]

Numerous other reports show the same. For examples:

> "Rapid border closures, full lockdowns, and wide-spread testing were not associated with COVID-19 mortality per million people."[146]

And,

> "The findings of this study suggest that prompt interventions were shown to be highly effective at reducing peak demand for intensive care unit (ICU) beds but also prolong the epidemic, in some cases resulting in more deaths long term. This happens because covid-19 related mortality is highly skewed towards older age groups. In the absence of an effective vaccination

---

[145] Yang E. "Experience From Other Countries Show Lockdowns Don't Work" AIER website. August 9, 2020

[146] Chaudry R, et al. "A country level analysis measuring the impact of government actions, country preparedness and socioeconomic factors on COVID-19 mortality and related health outcomes" Lancet EClinicalMedicine website. July 21, 2020

programme, none of the proposed mitigation strategies in the UK would reduce the predicted total number of deaths below 200,000."[147]

In October, when the Trump opposition was revving up the casedemic fearmongering in hopes of sputtering the economic recovery before the election, the bogus PCR "cases" were on the rise. This prompted the U.K., Germany, Spain, etc. to reinstitute lockdowns. Then, the all-knowing experts at The W.H.O. finally admitted that lockdowns are a bad idea:

"WHO envoy Dr. David Nabarro said such restrictive measures should only be treated as a last resort, the British magazine the Spectator reported in a video interview.

"We in the World Health Organization do not advocate lockdowns as the primary means of control of this virus," Nabarro said.

"The only time we believe a lockdown is justified is to buy you time to reorganize, regroup, rebalance your resources, protect your health workers who are exhausted, but by and large, we'd rather not do it."

Nabarro said tight restrictions cause significant harm, particularly on the global economy.

"Lockdowns just have one consequence that you must never, ever belittle, and that is making poor people an awful lot poorer," he said."[148]

---

[147] Rice K, et al. "Effect of school closures on mortality from coronavirus disease 2019: old and new predictions" BMJ website. October 7, 2020

[148] Salo J. "WHO warns against COVID-19 lockdowns due to economic damage" The New York Post website. October 11, 2020

But this was too little too late. The W.H.O. led the global lockdown strategy (after first denying that the virus was dangerous) after Tony Virus got the ball rolling. Their crimes against humanity have been perpetrated and cannot be undone. The dead cannot be revived. The bankruptcies cannot be cured.

Chapter 13: Reforms Needed to Prevent Future Scamdemics

The Wuhan virus scamdemic has set some extremely dangerous precedents that need to be reversed as soon as President Trump and the Republican Congress take over, should they win in November. If quick action is not taken, this new atomic weapon of politics, the scamdemic, will take root and become abused again and again.

This time, a virus pandemic was exploited by the left. However, there is nothing to prevent it from being exploited by a right next time. The lefties had better be careful because they unleashed a weapon that will come back to bite them.

The Marxists pretending to be racial justice warriors (i.e. the Black Lives Matter anarchists comprised mostly of white people) have called our nation's bluff. They exposed that the United States Constitution is just a piece of paper. Few were willing to defend it, not even Chief Justice Roberts.

The First Amendment has been rendered meaningless. The Supreme Court ruled repeatedly in 2020 that state leaders can do whatever they want regarding arbitrary lockdown orders, even if they clearly apply only to places of worship and not to casinos or large riots in the streets.

The Supreme Court has also repeatedly ruled that states have the right to arbitrarily issue decrees that drastically harm their citizens. The result has been a culling of humans in the case of nursing homes and the loss of livelihood for millions of others. School children and college kids have had their lives permanently altered by the arbitrary politically motivated decisions.

The lockdowns instituted to "flatten the curve" have not a scintilla of science to support them. The CDC dropped the ball. It is the agency created specifically to "control diseases" and yet it utterly failed.

At the NIH, Anthony Fauci epitomized the Deep State permanent bureaucrat. He was never elected to anything, yet somehow was given immense powers to shut down global economies. The boss of Anthony Fauci, Francis Collins, also has been in power far too long. The NIH and the CDC are corrupted to the core. Major restructuring is needed.

How can we fix the damage done? Can we prevent it from ever happening again?

The first step would be to pass legislation against lockdowns. There should be federal acts that make it illegal to shut down businesses and mandate personal protective equipment because there is no scientific justification for it all. In fact, the results of this global experiment are coming in now and countries with the least restrictive lockdowns had the fastest recovery and reached herd immunity, all while avoiding mass carnage that the fearmongers claimed would happen.

Then, there needs to be some sort of federal statue or Supreme Court ruling that allows the Department of Justice to take over cities that have run amok, such as Seattle, Portland, and New York did. All of the governors and mayors of those bodies clearly broke their oaths of office for political means. It should be possible to oust a bad mayor like Bill DeBlasio in the same way that they recall leaders in California or Washington.

The first step toward putting this nation back on the right track will occur on election day, November 3rd. There should be a purging of congress. Both parties are guilty. Also, the weak Republican governors caved in to pressures for lockdowns. They too should be ousted, starting with Ohio's Mike DeWine and Texas' Greg Abbott.

Then, the Department of Justice needs to arrest the billionaire communists who orchestrated the scamdemic sedition, such as Michael Novogratz, George Soros, and Bill Gates. The roundup should include the CEO's of the globalist conglomerates who own the propaganda news media and social media companies. We need an Attorney General willing to prosecute treason and sedition.[149]

And finally, that corrupt media was the tool used to spread the fear and drive the lockdowns. It is not First Amendment protected speech to yell fire in a movie theater. There should be laws that make it easier to sue a media source if they improperly report on any viral outbreak. Trial lawyers would be the only group willing to get the job done.

2020 was one of the darkest years for The United States of America. It exposed many of the festering problems caused by corporate and political corruption. Is there a silver lining to this cloud? Will this American experience all be cathartic or will it be the final nail on the coffin for democracy?

Can we recover and be better for it? Hopefully, what does not kill us will make us stronger.

---

[149] Moore M. "Top HHS spokesman accuses CDC staffers of 'sedition' over coronavirus: report" The New York Post website. September 14, 2020

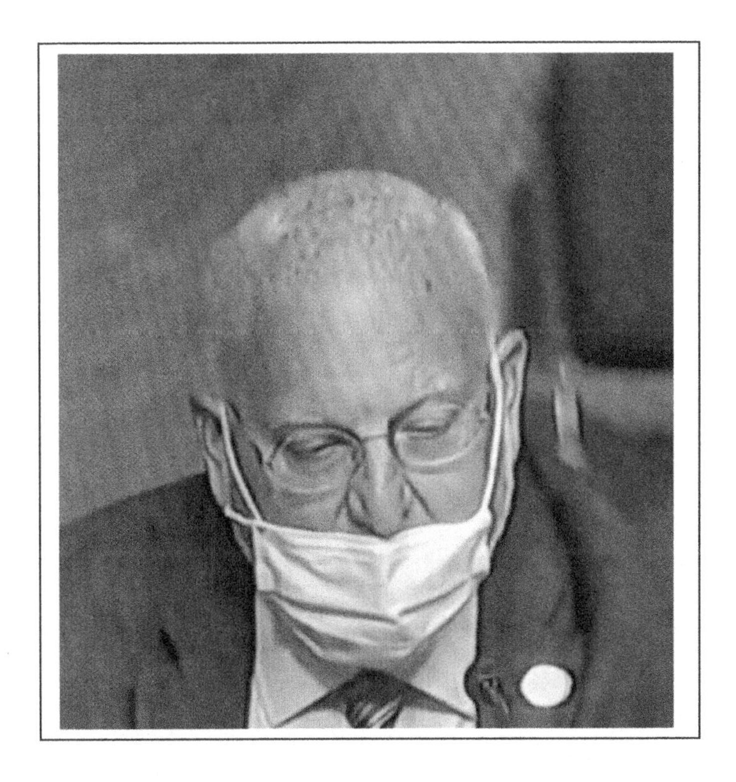

This iconic photo sums of the incompetence of the CDC and the entire scamdemic. It is the Director of the CDC, Robert Redfield, MD telling a congressional committee on September 16, 2020 that masks are more effective than vaccines, while using the wrong type of mask and wearing it improperly as well.

Essays

The following essays were written for my GreerJournal.com and book *Rules to Stop Radicals*. I hope you find them interesting.

The Human Population has Already Reached the Herd Immunity State for The Wuhan Virus

July 23, 2020- by Steven E. Greer, MD

As the propagandists in the mainstream media continue their full-court-press of fearmongering, desperately trying to prevent more months of record jobs employment numbers and quick rebound to the virus shutdown, something else is happening. Instead of the "surge in new cases" the press wants us to believe, the opposite is true. The virus seems to have run into the herd immunity brick wall, meaning the pandemic is over.

The Atlantic reported on Harvard researchers who used chaos theory math to build models estimating what portion of the population infected would be required to deliver herd immunity and stop the pandemic. They are coming up with a low number of only 20%. This means that New York City has already reached herd immunity, which is consistent with the latest data from the White House and New York showing no increase in deaths. Then, Oxford University professor Sunetra Gupta, who specializes in theoretical models of pandemics, who was the first to refute the wildly inflated estimates of death by Neil Ferguson, was interviewed. She stated, "According to scientific research, between 30 and 81 percent of the global population have T-cells from previous colds and flus that could automatically recognize the threat of the coronavirus, making them immune.

A large number of Australians will also be asymptomatic if they came down with the virus.

Professor Gupta argued it would be better to let COVID-19 spread in the community and have stronger measures to protect the vulnerable – such as the elderly or sick.

'You can only lock down for so long unless you choose to be in isolation for eternity so that's not a good solution,' she was quoted saying."

In a different interview with Gupta, "It's the biggest question in the world right now: is Covid-19 a deadly disease that only a small fraction of our populations have so far been exposed to? Or is it a much milder pandemic that a large percentage of people have already encountered and is already on its way out?

If Professor Neil Ferguson of Imperial College is the figurehead for the first opinion, then Sunetra Gupta, Professor of Theoretical Epidemiology at the University of Oxford, is the representative of the second. Her group at Oxford produced a rival model to Ferguson's back in March which speculated that as much as 50% of the population may already have been infected and the true Infection Fatality Rate may be as low as 0.1%.
As she sees it, the antibody studies, although useful, do not indicate the true level of exposure or level of immunity. First, many of the antibody tests are "extremely unreliable" and rely on hard-to-achieve representative groups. But more important, many people who have been exposed to the virus will have other kinds of immunity that don't show up on antibody tests — either for genetic reasons or the result of preexisting immunities to related coronaviruses such as the common cold.

The implications of this are profound – it means that when we hear results from antibody tests (such as a forthcoming official UK Government study) the percentage who test positive for antibodies is not necessarily equal to

the percentage who have immunity or resistance to the virus. The true number could be much higher.
Observing the very similar patterns of the epidemic across countries around the world has convinced Professor Gupta that it is this hidden immunity, more than lockdowns or government interventions, that offers the best explanation of the Covid-19 progression:

"In almost every context we've seen the epidemic grow, turn around and die away — almost like clockwork. Different countries have had different lockdown policies, and yet what we've observed is almost a uniform pattern of behavior which is highly consistent with the SIR model. To me that suggests that much of the driving force here was due to the build-up of immunity. I think that's a more parsimonious explanation than one which requires in every country for lockdown (or various degrees of lockdown, including no lockdown) to have had the same effect."
Asked what her updated estimate for the Infection Fatality Rate is, Professor Gupta says, "I think that the epidemic has largely come and is on its way out in this country so I think it would be definitely less than 1 in 1000 and probably closer to 1 in 10,000." That would be somewhere between 0.1% and 0.01%."

This is all more evidence that the current attempts in this country to "social distance" and prevent the spread of The Wuhan virus are not only unnecessary, but also counterproductive. No one else in the media is connecting the dots in this way. What Dr. Gupta and others are telling us is that this pandemic was, A) never dangerous to most people to begin with, and B) has reached herd immunity and is over.

Update July 30, 2020- Sweden has now reached the zero-death-rate.

Update August 3, 2020- I just did a radio segment on WLIR. Frank the host started the segment by playing an audio from Dr. Rand Paul from over the weekend. He was a guest on one of their shows (see video below).

Senator Paul used my essay reiterating that he thinks New York City has reached herd immunity. I won't bore you with the details, but it was 100% from my essay. No one was thinking this or writing about this before my essay. Even the scientists upon which I based my essay were not connecting the dots like this.

So, I have gotten this big idea rolling now. The world has reached herd immunity, meaning this virus is over. We are seeing it in Sweden, New York City, Germany, Italy, and other countries.

On the radio show, I facetiously said that I was going to predict when this pandemic would be over. I said November 4. That's the day after the election.

Update September 20, 2020- The WSJ has a lengthy report detailing how we have reached herd immunity. It is so similar to this essay that I have alerted their lawyers for a copyright infringement.

The Politics of Masks

August 14, 2020- by Steven E. Greer, MD

Topping the news today is Joe Biden's announcement that he would create a federal order mandating the wearing of face masks to somehow prevent deaths from the Wuhan virus. Actually, what he said was that he thinks there should be a federal mandate now, from Trump, but only for the next three-months, until the election. Well, at least he is honest about it. This is clearly a political stunt designed to support the notion that it is too dangerous to vote in person and mail-in ballots are required.

The idea for this announcement by Biden came from the polling that shows 70% of Americans would be in favor of a national mask mandate. But is that an accurate or misleading poll? Are Americans really perfectly fine with being forced to wear masks?

Currently, 16 states do not have mask mandates and they are all states with Republican governors. However, 10 other Republican states do have mask mandates. Ohio, Texas, West Virginia, Mississippi, Alabama, and Arkansas are states that voted for Trump and yet their governors have been Republicans in name only (RINO) when it comes to pandemic issues. Mike DeWine of Ohio and Gregg Abbott of Texas, for examples, have been fearmongering and harming the economy as much as the liberal states with governors scheming to hurt Trump by stalling his economy. Will those RINOs be rewarded or punished when they come up for re-election? Will Joe Biden score a win with his federal mask stunt?

This is what I think will happen. I think that Americans might answer a poll in a way to sound responsible, or simply be afraid to say what they really believe. I think that there is a strong disapproval for mask mandates and that most people who will vote are smart enough to know that the Democrats are fearmongering to hurt Trump. They look around and see no one falling ill at all, much less dying. They see the disconnect between the daily fearmongering propaganda and reality.

In states, such as Ohio, Texas, Alabama, Mississippi, and West Virginia, there has been a very low prevalence of illness caused by the Wuhan virus. The approval rating for Mike DeWine, for example, is very low among Trump voters because of his overreaction to the scamdemic. I think that many of these Republican governors of states with mask mandates will be voted out of office.

In the presidential election, what Biden says about anything does not matter. People are going to re-elect Trump with a wide margin of victory because the economy made a fast "V-shaped" recovery, people are sick and tired of the scamdemic destroying their livelihoods and personal liberties, and most of the "likely voters" see the Black Lives Matter rioting and far-left strategies of the Democrats as a Marxist revolution.

Trump could turn the Biden mask comments against him with a judo move. He should emphasize that the states have the rights to govern how they see fit, and that no science shows that masks help reduce deaths in general populations. Trump should expose how the Democrats are trying to destroy millions of lives and the economy for the purpose of gaining power.

From here on, pretty much anything the lame Democrat strategists tell Biden to say can be used against them in a heartbeat. They are the same dimwits who got the Democrat party into this sad condition.

(Dr. Greer was the first person in the country to advocate on TV that masks could be an optional safety measure. Before that, he has advocated for masks to be worn during the regular flu season and on airplanes.)

Update August 25, 2020- That was fast. Ohio's legislature drafts articles of impeachment against Governor DeWine for his irrational lockdown and mask mandates. I told you so.

The Bolshevik Revolution 4.0

May 31, 2020– by Steven E. Greer

The press on the left and the right is doing such a bad job covering these riots. The TV news is nothing but sensational images of stores being gutted and skirmishes with police. There is no attempt to explain why and how this is all happening.

First, the "news" is failing to even attempt to identify the funding sources and who are organizing these non-spontaneous, planned, organized, riots. I am sure that we will ultimately learn far-left billionaires are behind it all, protected by layers of shell companies and non-profits.

Recall, people like George Soros, Tom Steyer, the Koch brothers, etc. first used paid stooges in Guatemala to send thousands of illegal immigrants in caravans designed to overrun the border. Then, they got their big break with the pandemic and took advantage of that. Using their propagandist puppets in the media and their corrupt Democrat leaders in state and city governments, they shut down the country with fearmongering.

The goal is to stir anarchy in hopes of destroying the country as we know it. This is nothing but the Bolshevik revolution of 100 years ago in its third form: The Bolshevik 4.0. This current revolution has all of the hallmarks of those in the past. It starts with extreme disparities in wealth with no middle-class. Then, power-hungry people come along, exploit that, and turn those angry people into their soldiers. And then, when it is all over, those same people used as front-line social warriors become slaves to the new tyrants, just as Lenin, Stalin, and all of the other communist leaders have done over the ages. In the process, there is absolutely nothing off-limits to achieve their goal of power. Anything justifies the means. Previous communist revolutions have killed tens of millions of people. So, what we are seeing now, which is merely a little bit of rioting and a shutdown of an economy, is child's play to them.

The media are also failing to connect the dots. Much of the fuel for these riots is coming from three-months of house-arrest. This is what you get when you take peoples' livelihoods away and tell them that they cannot even touch one another.

Far-left NeverTrump Propaganda has Hijacked the Peer-Review Process

June 3, 2020- by Steven E. Greer, MD

We are living in surreal dystopian times. The far-left NeverTrump revolution has already scared the globalist corporations into compliance. Now, they have also managed to get their boots on the neck of the once-hallowed medical literature peer-reviewed industry (which, of course, is funded by the large drug companies and very much part of the establishment opposing populism and President Trump).

The large medical journals, such as Lancet, NEJM, JAMA, and other industry-funded sources have long been a venue for junk-science. The journals look the other way when statistical trickery is used to inflate efficacy, for example. Now, they are publishing woefully unworthy "studies" designed to hurt Trump. They have been rendered into classic textbook propaganda by the fascists behind the Wizard of Oz curtain.

On May 25, 2020 the Lancet and NEJM published papers that used a global coronavirus patient registry to conclude that hydroxychloroquine posed a safety hazard. It triggered the World Health Organization to halt their trials underway around the world. I promptly pointed out that such a database had to be unreliable and, therefore, the papers were junk-science. I was right.

The Guardian newspaper investigated and found that a shady American company called Surgisphere was behind the mysterious database used by the medical authors. However, the company seems to be a total fraud created to give the appearance of a global medical records company. In fact, it has six employees and they are not scientists. One even seems to be a porn actor. It is entirely possible that the World Health Organization, which is highly political and battling President Trump at the moment, paid Surgisphere to create a fake database, much like the infamous Steele dossier that the Democrats funded to dig up dirt on Trump.

As a result, the Lancet and NEJM seem to be planning to retract the papers. The Guardian reports, "Late on Tuesday, after being approached by the Guardian, the Lancet released an "expression of concern" about its published study. The New England Journal of Medicine has also issued a similar notice."

On May 7, 2020, the NEJM published online a paper, "Observational Study of Hydroxychloroquine in Hospitalized Patients with Covid-19" authored by doctors from far-left Columbia University that concluded, "This study does not support the use of hydroxychloroquine" However, the "study" they conducted was nothing that normally would have been published it the NEJM. It was an observational study that aimed to determine whether the drug helped ICU patients.

But rather than measure meaningful parameters, such as fever, percent of patients discharged, etc., the Upper Manhattan Columbia University investigators created a clinically meaningless composite endpoint of "need for ventilator or death". Well, the decision of when to use a ventilator is highly subjective. A large nearby medical system, Northwell Health, is investigating if their hospitals overused and mismanaged ventilators resulting in deaths. Therefore, if both the decision to use a ventilator is subjective, and ventilators can also contribute to death[150], then the composite endpoint of this study is meaningless because of the bias.

---

[150] Wright, J. "Doctors' haste to put coronavirus patients on mechanical ventilators during the pandemic's first wave may have RAISED the death rate, medic says" Daily Mail UK website. October 19, 2020

In fact, one could easily imagine that the strange composite endpoint was created by the investigators as a way to engineer an outcome of the "study" in order to justify the high death rates in those hospitals. The number of Wuhan virus deaths in New York were many times greater, per capita, than any other large city. New York hospitals, due to pressure by Governor Cuomo, were not offering hydroxychloroquine in most cases. Therefore, if a junk-science medical publication were to conclude that the drug had no benefit, as these authors did, then that would be quite convenient indeed. Hmm.

I asked the lead author, Neil Schluger, for comment several times. He refused to even reply. Likewise, Sinclair Broadcasting reporter Sharyl Attkisson did her own story on the numerous so-called trials bashing hydroxychloroquine, and she too could not get a single author to comment.

Now, making the news today is a supposedly well-designed, randomized, placebo-controlled, trial on hydroxychloroquine in the prevention or prophylaxis indication. That got my attention. The study was designed to test whether or not the drug reduced the transmission of the coronavirus among a cohort that had close-contact with known-infected patients. However, upon reviewing the paper, the trial failed to properly measure the only parameter that was important to measure, which was the virus-test-positive status of the patients.

In most patients followed in the study, the investigators failed to test the trial subjects in the cohorts for the actual virus! Instead, they used the highly subjective process of clinical diagnosis. Not only did that method of study design certainly create a high false-positive rate, but it also ignored the asymptomatic people who contracted the virus. We know that most people with the SARS-CoV-2 Wuhan coronavirus never even know they have it.

Before today, it would have been hard for me to imagine such a study being published anywhere, much less in the prestigious NEJM. It would be like publishing a study testing a cancer drug that used clinical examination to measure the tumor rather than pathology specimens or radiology.

The authors admitted their shortcomings in the discussion section: "Although PCR or serologic testing for asymptomatic infection would have added to the scientific strength of this trial, this was not possible, and we cannot assess an effect on mild or asymptomatic infections. Although a marginal possible benefit from prophylaxis in a more at-risk group cannot be ruled out…We acknowledge that this trial has limitations. Because of the lack of availability of diagnostic testing in the United States, the vast majority of the participants, including health care workers, were unable to access testing."

This study did achieve one thing. It showed that hydroxychloroquine is safe. Despite the NeverTrump propaganda claiming that the drug is "deadly", there were no increases in heart dysrhythmia or any other serious adverse event.

The only study underway, to my knowledge, that could answer this question of whether hydroxychloroquine is safe and also effective at prophylaxis is being conducted at Henry Ford Hospital in Detroit. Results should be ready in July.

What is clear is that the long-troubled medical peer-review publication process has now been hijacked by the far-left revolution that wants to change the world order. If it means demonizing a life-saving medication in order to hurt the chances of President Trump being re-elected, then so be it.

Update June 4, 2020- The fraudulent authors of the Lancet paper have retracted it and blame Surgisphere. In fact, Lancet and the authors had to have known that it was too good to be true to have a treasure trove of clinical data on coronavirus patients taking hydroxychloroquine.

There needs to be an investigation into the editors of Lancet and these authors for ties to the W.H.O. Did the anti-Trump W.H.H. pay for Surgisphere data ala the Democrats paying for the bogus Steel dossier?

Until this is sorted out, all reputable doctors should boycott Lancet and the NEJM. Don't hold your breath.

Update June 4, 2020-Shortly after the Lancet, the NEJM also retracted their publication of this fraudulent report. The editors stated:

"Because all the authors were not granted access to the raw data and the raw data could not be made available to a third-party auditor, we are unable to validate the primary data sources underlying our article, "Cardiovascular Disease, Drug Therapy, and Mortality in Covid-19."[1] We therefore request that the article be retracted. We apologize to the editors and to readers of the *Journal* for the difficulties that this has caused.

Mandeep R. Mehra, M.D.
Brigham and Women's Hospital Heart and Vascular Center, Boston, MA
mmehra@bwh.harvard.edu

Sapan S. Desai, M.D., Ph.D.
Surgisphere, Chicago, IL

SreyRam Kuy, M.D., M.H.S.
Baylor College of Medicine, Houston, TX

Timothy D. Henry, M.D.
Christ Hospital, Cincinnati, OH

Amit N. Patel, M.D.
University of Utah, Salt Lake City, UT

This letter was published on June 4, 2020, at NEJM.org."

Update June 4, 2020- The blast email platform we use, Mailchimp, which is owned by Big Tech company The Rocket Science Group LLC, promptly shut down our account for sending this story. There was no explanation given.

Update June 8, 2020- Amit N. Patel, M.D., one of the NEJM authors, has been fired

Exploitation of a Pandemic with House-Arrest Orders Allowed the Anarchists to Take Over

June 9, 2020- by Steven E. Greer

Last week, when the shockingly good June employment numbers hit, showing that 2.5 million jobs were added and the unemployment rate actually fell a point, the "news" went into full propaganda mode trying to spin the data in a negative way. They even resorted to insinuating that President Trump cooked the books. Why was the left so afraid of these numbers?

As people become employed after the pandemic house-arrest orders lift, they also become ineligible to participate in radical movements. It would be interesting to know the unemployment rate of the people who marched last weekend across the country. The majority of them were likely unemployed and disenfranchised. Ironically, the groups pretending to be the angriest, such as Antifa, Black Lives Matter, Democrat officials, "community organizers", college professors, and teachers were all cashing paychecks.

In the month of June, there will likely be another 5 to 10 million people re-employed. That is also so many people who can no longer participate in the radical movements. The window of opportunity to create anarchy and oust Trump is shrinking fast.

Therefore, the pandemic fearmongers will be back trying to revive the mass house-arrest orders. In the Apple iPhone newsfeed today, numerous propaganda stories from the Atlantic and so forth "report" that the virus will never go away and that we are recklessly opening up the country too soon:

- Coronavirus outbreak may take up to 5 years to come under control: WHO
- WHO says coronavirus pandemic far from over as world sees largest daily increase
- WHO warns the pandemic is worsening across the globe
- The original Sars virus disappeared – here's why coronavirus won't do the same
- Arizona's Spike in COVID-19 Cases 'Definitely Related' to Reopening
- CBS: As summer nears, coronavirus concerns grow
- CBS: Health officer who mandated face masks resigns after threats
- The Atlantic Daily: The Protests Meet the Pandemic: Neither appears to be abating. Today, we're examining where they intersect.
- Anthony Fauci warns "worst nightmare" pandemic is not even close to being over

This unprecedented communist-party-like anarchy in our country is made possible only by the equally historic oppression of the people for four months with the pandemic house-arrest orders. It was a recipe for an uprising of the masses.

George Floyd's murder was just the spark to light the bonfire and the professional agitators are throwing wood on the pile. All of the large protests seen last weekend were manned by newly-unemployed people who were sick of being forced inside. They were tired of bickering with family members and staring at the walls. The hate spewed on TV stoked their anger. Now, those pressures have burst like a balloon as the country reopens. So too will the energy behind the Bolshevik Revolution 3.0 deflate.

Is Tony Fauci Looking for His Legacy in Vaccines?

August 6, 2020- by Steven E. Greer, MD

Here again is Tony Fauci hyping vaccines [referring to a video posted on GreerJournal.com that cannot be seen in here in print]. He is normally a doomsayer and fearmonger regarding the Wuhan virus. Why is he so hopeful on this one aspect of the pandemic?

In a 2011 Op-Ed in the Washington Post, Fauci rationalized why his labs should be allowed to create man-made dangerous viruses using genetic engineering. The euphemism he gives to this process is "gain-of-function" These viruses would be classified as Weapons of Mass Destruction and violate international law if they were used by the military. So, note how Fauci emphasizes the intent of his gain-of-function labs is to save lives by creating new drugs and vaccines.

Playing God in a virus lab: What could go wrong?

After the 2011 Op-Ed, Anthony Fauci and is infectious disease branch of the NIH funded several of these gain-of-function labs in the U.S. He even funded the actual Wuhan, China lab, which leaked the coronavirus. It is quite possible that these labs created the SARS-CoV-2 that is crippling the global economy.

Then, the program was shut down in 2014. Ebola became a huge problem for the World in 2014. A former scientist working in the Fauci labs claims that they created Ebola. She has been jailed and suffered a concerted effort to discredit her.

What can be confirmed is this: "Following controversy surrounding research, published in 2012, that led to the creation of highly pathogenic H5N1 (avian) influenza virus strains that were airborne transmissible between ferrets—and more recent reports of biosafety mishaps involving anthrax, smallpox, and H5N1 in government laboratories—in 2014 the administration of US President Barack Obama called for a "pause" on funding (and relevant research with existing US Government funding) of GOF experiments involving influenza, SARS, and MERS viruses in particular. This pause applies specifically to experiments that "may be reasonably anticipated to confer attributes … such that the virus would have enhanced pathogenicity and/or transmissibility in mammals via the respiratory route" (White House 2014)."

In 2017 under the new and confused Trump administration, taking advantage of the opportunity, Fauci restarted his pet project gain-of-function lab work in 2017. And now we have the release of the Wuhan virus from one of Fauci's labs. It is not confirmed that the virus was the product of the gain-of-function genetic engineering work or whether the lab simply housed cultures of the wild virus.

Is Fauci obsessed with creating drugs that work based on his decades-long desire to create man-made viruses? His own words in the 2011 Op-Ed make this clear. It would be his legacy if he can say that his research created the vaccine cure for this Wuhan virus pandemic.

There is only one small obstacle to Fauci's ego. Cheap, safe, effective, drugs can prevent the virus from spreading and cure those who contract it, thereby making a Fauci-cure less important. Corticosteroids and hydroxychloroquine (HCQ) are two of them.

Fauci's NIH has also funded many of the clinical trials for expensive new drugs to treat the Wuhan virus. Gilead's remdesivir is one of them. Those too would suffer in sales if HCQ worked just as well.

Not coincidentally, Fauci has been among the most vocal against the use of HCQ. Last week, his comments about HCQ being ineffective were based on a gross abuse of the data, which included the citation of Lancet and NEJM that have been retracted due to fraudulent data.

Clearly Tony Fauci wants his lab-funded vaccines to save the day rather than President Trump's HCQ.

The actual pandemic itself started with Fauci's fearmongering about the risks to attending large sporting events. In fact, the virus has had a death rate of 0.1% and is far less deadly than the regular flu to the vast majority of people. It certainly seems as if Fauci fearmongered a fake pandemic only to come along and save the day with his own lab-created therapies.

Tony Fauci is a small man by physical stature who grew up in tough New York. He tried to reinvent history this year by giving the press stories about his stellar high school basketball career. But the fact is that he is not an athlete (as seen in his first-pitch at the MLB Nationals game). He has also appeared to be the super-expert "scientist" on pandemics, but he has not performed any science for 40-years and is not an epidemiologist. Tony Fauci, never elected to any policy-making job, is a Deep State, partisan, Democrat hack reveling on his new-found power and fame.

All of Anthony Fauci's comments, that have held such sway over the world, have been highly biased and inaccurate. Little Tony Fauci, like Mighty Mouse, wants to be known as the man who saved the day and cured the pandemic with his vaccines. If that means withholding life-saving HCQ and other drugs, then so be it.

Anthony Fauci Unjustifiably Caused a Mass Panic

March 13, 2020- by Steven E. Greer, MD

With one sentence in response to a question from a congressional hearing, an obscure medical doctor caused a mass panic of unprecedented proportion. The doctor was 79-year-old Anthony Fauci, the head of the National Institute of Allergy and Infectious Diseases at the National Institutes of Health.

How did he do this? Was he correct or wrong in an epic way?

The Wall Street Journal reported, "Just two days ago, when a Republican congressman used his time in a public coronavirus briefing to ask [Dr. Fauci], he thought he would get a calming response. The Ivy League had recently canceled the rest of its season. The National Basketball Association was still playing in full arenas.

"Is the NBA underreacting," Rep. Glenn Grothman asked, "or is the Ivy League overreacting?"

The unsettling answer that Dr. Anthony Fauci offered to Congress changed everything over a dizzying 24 hours that will be remembered as the most extraordinary day for American sports in decades. "We would recommend that there not be large crowds," said Fauci, the director of the National Institute of Allergy and Infectious Disease, an expert who has been a fixture of American public health for nearly four decades. "If that means not having any people in the audience when the NBA plays, so be it."

Fauci's candid remarks caught the NBA and some Trump administration officials by surprise. But they were proven to be prescient almost immediately. By the end of Wednesday, the NBA season was not just spectator-less. It was suspended.

What happened in between was that Utah Jazz center Rudy Gobert tested positive for the virus and became forever known as the patient zero in American professional sports.

Less than a day after Fauci was in front of Congress answering questions about the NBA, the league had made the decision to shut itself down for at least 30 days, several teams were in self-quarantine, and the entire sports industry was being shaken to its core.

The NBA's action was the tipping point that prompted a wave of similar moves from other sports and shocked many Americans into paying attention to a global pandemic that has now disrupted everyday life in the U.S. The suspensions continued on Thursday with the National Hockey League, Major League Baseball and, the NCAA [March Madness] tournament" (and then the PGA Tour as well as The Masters).

Entire cities are now shutting down. New York has banned large crowds over 500-people in size. The subways might stop running. Most schools are shutting down indefinitely.

Was Dr. Fauci, acting as the "face of coronavirus", as a policymaker, correct in stating that large crowds should be avoided? The answer is an unequivocal "no".

There are no official epidemiology guidelines to warrant shutting down a nation for the level of threat that COVID-19 poses. If there were, the CDC should have been the agency to issue them, not an NIH bench lab researcher never confirmed by the senate.

There is no reason to view the COVID-19 coronavirus as being a deadly threat more dangerous that a myriad of other viruses that are amongst us all the time. As of March 13, there have been 40-deaths and 1,600 diagnosed cases in this country. All of the deaths have been people who were elderly or otherwise medically challenged form illness. The numbers from South Korea, where testing is far more prevalent, support a death rate of well under 1%. There is currently no reason to treat COVID-19 like a science fiction pandemic to kill half the population.

The reaction to this virus has set a dangerous precedent. Every year there are new strains of the flu, SARS, etc. that could cripple our economy if the incompetent and biased media politicized it. People die by the millions from infectious diseases. That is normal and unpreventable.

I have been following these virus pandemics for two-decades since I became a Wall Street analyst and money manager. When I ran the entire healthcare portfolio for Merrill Lynch in 2005, it was the avian "bird" flu that mobilized us. In 2009 and 2010, under President Obama, a genuine safety hazard spread in the form of Influenza sub-type H1N1, or "swine flu" That administration downplayed it as thousands of people died. The current COVID-19 is nothing like swine flu. It is far less virulent.

Dr. Fauci failed to factor in the gravitas of his words when he spoke before congress. He spoke irresponsibly.

Dr. Fauci is not a policymaker. He is not a senior member of Homeland Security or the military. He is a basic-science research nerd who gained fame with the HIV epidemic. He has since been running his fiefdom within the corrupt NIH for decades (The corruption of the NIH is beyond the scope of this essay). He is a government bureaucrat who pushes papers and directs your taxpayer dollars to go to the same Ivy League schools, year after year. Dr. Fauci has never been elected to anything. He has no leadership experience.

How is it then that such a non-leader was allowed to have such an impact on the United State and the world? If you want to blame Trump for something, this would be a fair criticism. Trump is, yet again, letting his cabinet run amok.

Actually, it was Republican senators who got the Trump administration to make Fauci the face of the epidemic. It should be of no surprise that the inept senate misled a clueless White House.

Now, President Trump is forced to deal with the hand dealt him. He could use jiu-jitsu and go even crazier than the Democrats by shutting down the nation with a state of emergency. By doing so, he would then be able to take credit for "preventing" a deadly pandemic. Of course, there will be no way to disprove him. He can also take advantage of the false crisis and get some tax cuts passed.

Stay tuned to see how President Trump deals with the false panic induced by Anthony Fauci.

Update: One-hour after posting this article, President Trump and VP Pence sure seemed to demote Anthony Fauci on live TV with a new, better spoken, less hand-wringing, smart as hell, woman doctor.

Steven E Greer, MD Causes Tony Fauci, MD to Retract his Estimates of Virus Deaths

April 6, 2020- by Steven E. Greer, MD

I was the first person to point out that Tony Fauci, MD, the unquestionable guru who had the morons in the media subdued like headlights to a deer, was in fact bluffing and making it up when he estimated that 200,000 people would die from the coronavirus. I based this on my decades of experience at making predictive models at the highest levels of Wall Street.

I repeated my essay on the Joe Piscopo radio show. Then, a few days later on Friday, Fox News' Tucker Carlson ran a long segment on the same topic (i.e. that Fauci's models were unreliable and that his irresponsible comments led to the closure of the American economy, causing more than 10 million people to file for unemployment (so far) and 700,000 jobs to be lost in March).

Today, on Monday, the dominoes that I set in motion took their toll on Chicken Little Fauci. When asked whether he stood by those fearmongering estimates, he backed down (see video above).

Fauci tried to revise history and say that his comments were based on the data at the time. Well, that is false. His comments were not based on any models at all and he said them to spread fear and manipulate governors and the President of the United States to close down the country. Fauci is a permanent bureaucrat Democrat who was being encouraged by the far-left to destroy Trump's economy. He was drunk with power.

Tony Fauci needs to be held accountable. There needs to be hearings to look into his communications with the Democrats and what his true motivations were. Regardless, he must be fired.

The New York Virus Death Rates are Too High. Why?

March 29, 2020- by Steven E. Greer, MD

I have been following closely the death rates from this SARS-CoV-2 virus, also known as COVID-19, or simply as coronavirus. I thought that the rates would drop below 1% as more people were tested. Well, they have been increasing, and are now at 1.76%. Why?

Upon closer inspection, those death rates are greatly skewed by the hot-spot of New York, with the city being the source of most of the cases for the entire state. If one takes those deaths out of the spreadsheet, then the national death rate is 1.15%.

Why have coronavirus deaths in New York City doubled over the last 48-hours? What is going on at the granular level?

There are only a handful of hospitals treating the majority of the virus patients. They are in the boroughs of Brooklyn and Queens, not in the gentrified wealthy parts.

Elmhurst Hospital has been at the epicenter of the coronavirus epidemic in New York. The Guardian reported, "Under normal circumstances, Elmhurst has a 15-bed intensive care unit. Now, it is full with Covid-19 patients who require invasive intubation to be on ventilators. As of Thursday morning, 45 of the hospital's now 63 ventilators were in use, a person with knowledge of hospital inventory said. In the last 48 hours, 50 additional hospital staff have been sent to Elmhurst hospital, and 60 patients transferred elsewhere to try to alleviate the strain on hospital staff. De Blasio said he is transferring another 40 ventilators to the hospital."

Elmhurst Hospital is located in a region of Queens where Latino immigrants comprise the majority of the population. Most of the patients under normal times are covered by Medicaid, if they have any insurance at all.

Despite those shortcomings as being one of the least equipped, least funded, least competent medical centers, Elmhurst has become the "center of excellence" where infected patients are being sent, and where ventilators are being shipped. At the same time, CEO's of the swanky Manhattan hospital, Mount Sinai, were exposed in the press for hiding out in Palm Beach in their multi-million-dollar second-homes as they collect salaries in excess of $6 Million.

One can see how eager the best medical centers in the city are to have virus patients sent to them by watching cable TV news. Fox News' Mark Siegel, MD, an NYU Langone doctor, was urging early on for sick patients to stay away from the hospital because the doctors were afraid of contracting the virus. He does his reporting from the safety of his apartment. Likewise, Nicole Saphier, a Memorial Sloan Kettering radiologist, reports with full makeup and a glowing smile from the safety of her home. Claiming that she is at high-risk from a "medication", Dr. Saphier is not going into the hospital. The only real doctor on the front-lines to appear on Fox News has been an Elmhurst ICU doctor, Sotirios Kassapidis, MD. (I stopped watching the other channels, but I am sure that ABC's Dr. Ashton, Dr. Oz, and CBS' Dr. Agus are all as bad.).

When thousands were killed by the 9/11 terrorist attacks 18-years ago, Bellevue Hospital in Manhattan was Command Central. If the President of the United States were to be shot while in New York, they would be treated at Bellevue if they were in Manhattan. When Ebola patients needed care in the city, they went to Bellevue. Now, Bellevue is not the "Center of Excellence" for this historic epidemic. Why?

Stephanie Guzman, A media spokesperson for the New York HHC that runs Bellevue and Elmhurst would not provide patient number for each hospital.

On March 14th, it was reported that the first New Yorker to die from the virus was treated at Brooklyn's Wyckoff Heights Medical Center. I know that facility well, having briefly moonlighted there in 1998 while doing research as a surgery resident at NYU. The facility itself was fine. It was not filthy, despite being in a low-income neighborhood. However, the senior doctors and executives were incompetent.

Fourteen-years later, in 2012, I began reading stories from the New York Time's Anemona Hartocollis about scandals of corruption at Wyckoff, none of which surprised me. For example, the hospital had established a special bank account for the purpose of providing bribes to a New York State Assemblyman who oversaw the hospital.

I reached out to Anemona Hartocollis and assisted her with some of the stories as well as submitted an Op-Ed. However, her gutless editors found my comments to be too harsh and it was not accepted.

Ms. Hartocollis replied to my email submission of the Op-Ed, "Steven: It's an interesting piece, but I don't think the OpEd page will publish a piece raising potentially damaging information about individuals like Dr. Gourji and Dr. Rao without giving them a chance to respond – a process that's normally done in a news story. I could pass it on, but I just don't think it meets Times standards for that reason. So your best bet, if you want to try anyway, is to send to oped@nytimes.com. They really do read every submission and if they are interested, will provide feedback. best, anemona"

Here is an excerpt from my submitted Op-Ed:

"When I was a surgery resident many years ago, I "moonlighted" part-time at Wyckoff Heights Hospital in Brooklyn while I took time off from residency training in

Manhattan to conduct clinical research trials. Compared to the large tertiary care teaching hospitals to which I was accustomed, Wyckoff Heights struck me even back then, before the scandals erupted, as being an institution run by corrupt and incompetent staff.

The Chief of the pediatric emergency department at Wyckoff, Dr. Sol Gourji, had failed his specialty medical board exams many times. The Chief of Surgery at Wyckoff, until his resignation in December of 2011, was Dr. A.C. Rao. He hired the part-time staff to moonlight and gave them responsibilities for which they were not trained. For example, the jobs of handling complex orthopedic fractures, and even neurosurgery emergencies, were given to doctors with no training in those specialties.

Since my time as a moonlighting surgeon, Wyckoff has become the most publicized of the corrupt and unsafe Brooklyn hospitals being investigated by Governor Cuomo's teams. Dr. Rao resigned in December, 2011, amidst investigations into unethical business practices. He was also part of the hospital board which is under fire. Dr. Gourji still practices to this day, despite never having passed his board exams.

A recent New York Times lengthy article detailed how a 22-year-old female patient, Sabrina Seelig, died in the Wyckoff Heights Medical Center ER after she was sedated without proper oxygen monitoring. She stopped breathing long enough to become brain dead, and later died.

Matters of financial graft and corruption aside, this type of unsafe and incompetent care is commonplace in these neglected hospitals that mostly treat the uninsured in New York City. I personally witnessed inexcusable healthcare delivery at Wyckoff in the few months that I worked there."

Governor Cuomo's staff has been "investigating" numerous failing and corrupt hospitals in New York's outer boroughs. His solution has been to pump more money into them and keep the zombies alive.

Now, these same hospitals, that are incompetent at best and corrupt at worst, are the "Centers of Excellence" treating critically ill coronavirus patients who need cutting edge medications never tried before in the country. What could go wrong?

This is why we are seeing carnage from the coronavirus. The wrong hospitals are treating the patients because the fancy Manhattan medical centers do not want the infection risks.

Governor Cuomo has been integrally involved in the failed attempts to clean up these very same hospitals. The blame falls squarely on his shoulders.

At the federal level, Anthony Fauci, MD of the NIH has been the most vocal about how we should handle this pandemic. However, he has not visited New York to inspect the problem. From his ivory tower in Washington, he seems to have been unable to spot all of the above; The wrong hospitals are treating these patients.

President Trump needs to take control of this crisis from Governor Cuomo. There needs to be an emergency medical center dedicated to the treatment of this virus. Perhaps the new facility at the Javits center, or the floating Navy hospitals, could do the job.

If each virus patient received hydroxychloroquine plus azithromycin, and/or received remdesivir, and/or immunoglobulin harvested from the plasma of people who have recovered, all of which would be overseen by competent doctors, then few people should die from SARS-C0V-2. At the same time, if healthy healthcare providers volunteered to take the vaccine that is now ready, to test the safety, it could be rolled out in full scale within months.

The status quo is unacceptable. Unqualified doctors are currently acting as ICU experts in underfunded, ill-equipped, hospitals that cannot treat even run-of-the-mill medical problems. This is why the death rates are increasing.

(Note: I applied to the state website that is recruiting doctors for New York and no one replied. I have also flown to New York recently as the fear was spreading.)

Update April 27, 2020

Holy cow. I was right and the care being delivered in these Queens hospitals is ten-times worse than I imagined. A nurse posted a video (see above). She is reliable and nothing she said seems unbelievable. This is not a hoax video.

In it, she states that the hospitals are:

A) Not giving hydroxychloroquine, Z-pack, Zinc, or

B) They certainly are not giving any of the experimental drugs like remdesivir,

C) Ventilators are just perfunctory ass-covering maneuvers to expedite death,

D) Doctors and nurses are not trained on the vents. In most cases, less invasive CPAP could be offered, which is less damaging to the lungs, but they prefer a closed-loop system of the vent to avoid spreading the virus, they reason. But is is all just cowardice. They will not even perform chest compressions during a code in fear of the virus.

E) The quack-cowards are not even entering hospital ICU rooms with ventilators active, in fear of the virus.

F) Hundreds of out-of-town nurses are sitting in hotels, paid for by FEMA, and the overloaded hospitals are keeping them out.

The hospitals do not want outsiders to see this. They do not want help because their goal is to kill them and avoid costly rehab that the state cannot afford? Who knows what is the motivation. It is likely a combination of misguided euthanasia, *ala* the nursing home massacre in New Orleans after Hurricane Katrina, with some political incompetence added on top like a cherry to this clusterfuck sundae.

The nurse echoes my essay. She said that these hospitals were "crappy" even before the virus challenges hit them. I worked there back in the late 90's moonlighting. I spotted this a month ago.

Israel Rocha, a congressional staffer, is the CEO of Elmhurst Hospital. If that is not the unnamed hospital in the video, it is nearby. Wyckoff Heights Hospital is the other death camp.

Politically, this is 100% the fault of Cuomo, as I explained in my essay. It is consistent with Cuomo's other "just kill them" strategy of sending infected elderly back to nursing homes to infect others. Trump's administration is also to blame. They know all of the above and do not want to own the problem if they touch it. This is why the Javits and the floating hospital ship went unused. The Feds did not want to own it.

During the Obamacare debates, the Republicans fearmongered "death panels". This is much worse. This is active murder we are seeing in NYC. That is not hyperbole or rhetoric.

Coronavirus is a New York Problem, Not a National Problem

April 19, 2020- by Steven E. Greer, MD

The nation has started the process of lifting home-quarantine orders and people have started to return to Florida beaches and New York golf courses. As this happens, there will be widely varying perspectives from Americans living in New York as compared to South Dakota. Those still under house arrest will be justifiably envious.

The mainstream media is clustered inside the Manhattan Bubble, where there is no hint of a lifting of the home-quarantine orders, and will be spewing more and more opinion pieces aimed at making the rest of America seem like hayseed country bumpkin morons for going back to normality. Are they correct or are they misguided and dishonest?

The dirty little secret that everyone knows inside Cuomo's offices in Albany, Manhattan hospital board rooms, and City Hall is that the high death rate is being generated from focal hot spots within Queens and other outer boroughs where Third World conditions have existed for centuries. This is not a national pandemic worthy of shutting down the global economy. This is a New York problem that can be further isolated as a problem of hot spots within Queens, etc.

As of today, 46% of all national deaths have come from New York (17,000 out of 37,000). Most of the new daily cases are from New York.

It is unknown precisely where the deaths have occurred because the New York City health department is covering up the mortality rates per hospital. New York has provided hospital-based mortality rates for decades and now has suddenly stopped doing this.

As previously detailed, a handful of hospitals outside of Manhattan have been so poorly managed, with many examples of frank corruption, that Governor Cuomo considered shutting them down. The NY Times has covered this story for decades. However, Cuomo, in his infinite wisdom, chose to throw $8 Billion at the dumpster fires. To deflect from his own shortcomings, Governor Cuomo has doubled down on his criticism of the federal government and President Trump.

These same hospitals are now the ones treating most of the coronavirus patients. The staff are heroes risking their lives, but their managers are incompetent and corrupt. The doctors staffing these hospitals are not the best. It is hard to find competent doctors to work in these hospitals.

In addition to poor medical care, the overall conditions in these neighborhoods are the same as any Third World country in South America. In fact, most of the residents are immigrants from those regions and have no private insurance. These are Medicaid neighborhoods and our corrupt American healthcare system favors private insurance (read The Medical Advocate).

New York is not just the biggest city in the country. It also has the widest variety and highest concentrations of immigrants without proper healthcare. Elsewhere, patients with any type of illness, including coronavirus, receive night and day different care. The populations outside of New York City are also far less concentrated, making it harder for infectious diseases to spread.

This coronavirus causing the pandemic, technically known to scientists as SARS-CoV-2 (not COVID-19, which is a nonsense term created by the W.H.O.), is far less virulent than the 1918 Spanish flu that killed 500,000 Americans and 30 Million around the world. The Spanish flu killed the youngest and strongest of people. People would first suffer symptoms and then die within 12-hours. Their skin changed color to black and blue. Their noses spewed blood. It was much more like the recent Ebola outbreak. In contrast, this coronavirus selectively kills certain populations with underlying medical ailments. The young and healthy almost always survive or even fail to know they were sick at all. The overall death rate will certainly come down once the true prevalence of the virus is determined.

Our leaders have overreacted to this epidemic. They were led over the cliff by the fearmongering of Anthony Fauci who pretended to have accurate scientific models predicting 200,000 deaths when he really had nothing. He was bluffing. Despite the retrospective claims that "mitigation" and "social distancing" are the reasons deaths were lower than expected, there is not a shred of scientific evidence support that. It is simply propaganda by the people who created this man-made catastrophe (the virus was man-made in China and the overreaction leading to the global depression was man-made).

As a result of the draconian unconstitutional actions by our federal and state leaders, trillions of dollars of assets have been lost globally. Real homes and small businesses have been taken away from people who had thriving businesses just two-months ago. The Paycheck Protection Program and other stimulus plans have failed to help the vast majority suffering. There are already long lines at food pantries around the country. True suffering greater than that seen in the 1930's is upon us.

The United States of America is a culture that values liberty over life. The slogan "Give me liberty of give me death" says it all. The small risk to the nation from coronavirus does not warrant the suspension of our liberties.

This false-pandemic has been nothing but an excuse for the far-left in their ivory towers to turn a crisis into a social agenda opportunity. They sit around all day long scheming grand theories of remaking the world order.

Of note, President Woodrow Wilson was one of these elites. He was the President of Princeton before becoming POTUS. He first led the nation into futile World War One purely due to his huge ego and grand theory to remake the Western World under his 14-point plan. Then, the Spanish flue came along and was treated as an inconvenience to his plans. He ordered is propaganda soldiers to stifle coverage of the deaths. He had no federal policy to "social distance" He packed hundreds of thousands of healthy Americans into ships to go to Europe knowing they would contract the Spanish flu.

Ironically, the flu killed so many people, and scared people away from the election booths, that Wilson lost the congress to the Republicans who derailed his efforts to shape Europe after the armistice. His own propaganda campaigns that stifled dissent also turned off his liberal base, ironically again.

For the academic elites, they view their idealism as divine intervention. Any mean justifies the end. Today, shutting down the global economy is a mere "inconvenience" according to Anthony Fauci, who will never lose his federal job under any circumstances.

Pay attention to every person in the media critical of reopening the country. None of them have jobs in jeopardy. They are elected officials or are somehow being paid by the taxpayer. Every pundit on the liberal TV shows is paid by grants from larger organizations.

Not only does the nation need to reopen immediately, but actions must be taken to prevent the government from doing this again. If not, it will be very easy to use the annual spread of disease as an excuse to alter elections and stage coups. The current governors who overreached the most must be ousted by armed mobs. Then, there needs to be a constitutional convention to update the laws of the land.

The Truly Scary Consequence of this "Pandemic" is the Erosion of Our Civil Rights

April 2, 2020- by Steven E. Greer

Many months ago, when a news story caught my eye about how a New York City agency was trying to make it a crime to use the term illegal alien, I spotted that as the encroachment of fascism that is commonplace in the United Kingdom. Over there, if someone literally use the wrong adjective to describe Muslim immigrants, they can be thrown in jail for a "hate crime".

Of course, they have no first amendment or a bill of rights in the UK. Our constitution is powerful and will protect us, right? Think again.

The United States does not operate in a vacuum. Whatever political forces are surrounding us in the world have an influence on us too. When far-left radicals in this country see the UK and the rest of Europe get away with this oppression of free speech, they become emboldened here in the States.

Sure enough, because no one challenged the New York City law that banned the use of "illegal alien", with even Fox News ignoring for the most part, it has created copycats in other large cities. The police chief in Seattle proudly made a public announcement stating that her police department would arrest people if they used "hate speech" to discuss the coronavirus in terms of being Asian or Chinese in origin.

This scares the daylights out of me. For anyone with an independent mind who speaks the truth, we now have to be worried that some far-left communist district attorney, funded by George Soros and his ilk, will prosecute us. Would we eventually win after years of litigation in Federal Court? Probably. But in the meantime, our lives would be ruined.

All of this is happening as the far-left exploits this pandemic crisis. There are other concerning trends as well that are arising and the crisis is exploited.

In congress, the Democrats spot an opportunity to get their large spending programs passed. They are going to be pressing for another humongous multi-trillion-dollar package that would end up doing nothing but feeding the pension funds of states. They will call it "infrastructure spending" but the funds will just go onto the general funds of states and be gobbled up to pay for pensions.

Also, the fact that these state and local governments, with incompetent mayors and governors, have successfully corralled hundreds of millions of people into their homes like sheep, this will embolden them to take future steps to violate our civil rights. They will start looking towards home raids to confiscate guns, or any other thing that fits their agenda. They have called the bluff of America and they see that we will do whatever they tell us to do.

However, I am optimistic that far too many people agree with me. I do not think that people will stay at home much longer. In parts of the country where the virus is not a problem, such as in Florida, there will be an uprising. Today, under extreme pressure, the Florida governor closed golf courses. The only thing keeping people sane down here is that all of these retired folks can go out to the golf course. Now, there will be millions of old people stuck in their homes unable to do anything. I do not think that is going to last very long.

The Department of Justice, led by William Barr, has been derelict of its duty to enforce the constitution and our civil rights. When local corrupt DA's let violent criminals out of jail, or when a police chief chills our rights to free speech, the DOJ should be taking action. Instead, Barr has been in hiding.

President Trump needs to get a new Attorney General. Barr did his job, which was to kill the bogus Mueller probe. He now seems to lack the will to take on the Deep State. Some young gun with presidential aspirations, such as Missouri Senator Josh Hawley, needs to take over. The communists are using the pandemic crisis to strip us of our rights.

(Note: The statistical death rate numbers that are alarming Michigan and Florida are caused by hotspots in big cities just like New York. There is not a problem in Florida. There is a problem in Third World country Miami and Dade County. There is not a problem in Michigan. There is a problem in the extremely dysfunctional government of Detroit. President Trump needs to revisit his idea of quarantining certain cities, not the entire states).

The Government Needs Special Powers Over the Media During Pandemics

March 15, 2020- by Steven E. Greer, MD

Amy Acton, MD is Ohio Governor DeWine's coronavirus spokesperson. She was on Tucker Carlson with him to explain why they made the irresponsible fearmongering statement that 100,000 Ohioans have coronavirus.

But she seemed to be literally drunk. Dr. Acton blamed her bizarre behavior on sleep deprivation. To make a long story short, their rationale for claiming that 100,000 Ohioans have COVID-19 was totally unfounded. They simply took an estimated prevalence of one-percent and extrapolated to the Ohio population. However, they were misapplying those numbers. The one-percent number comes from hot spot areas of infection, not from a sampling of the entire population.

The impact of their statements came swiftly. Ohio shut down all events of 100 or more people. Schools shuttered, and so on. The media dissemination of these irresponsible comments from DeWine's office was the real weapon that did the damage.

The Republican leaders are scaring people to prevent coronavirus deaths from being used against them during the election, and it might just work. They are inconveniencing the country so much that the masses will demand to have their normal routine back. The Democrats will start to criticize them for overreacting, instead of under reacting, which is not a bad thing during election cycles. The GOP will claim they prevented a pandemic, which is impossible to disprove.

Had President Trump and his party not taken the lead at overreacting, the Democrats would have done it for them. If Trump *et al* had done very little, the Democrat propaganda machines would have filled the void. No good crisis goes without being exploited by the media and their political backers.

Meanwhile, billions of lost revenue, jobs, and inconveniences will take place. Our nation has been harmed greatly.

This is the big lesson: The government needs to have rare, narrowly-defined, powers to circumvent the First Amendment in cases of pandemics and ban coverage of the crises. Crying "fire" in a theater is not protected speech. Scaring people over pandemics is not protected speech either. I just orally argued this week in the Second Circuit my First Amendment case. I know what I am talking about.

There should be a special bipartisan, screened-before-airing, news operation during a pandemic. The White House would oversee it.

How would one enforce this? Easy: arrest the presidents of the news if they collude to fearmonger. Their staff are spineless sheep and would get in line quickly. The FBI could monitor the situation and gather evidence if the newsrooms were conspiring to fearmonger during morning news meetings, etc.

Obviously, the government cannot be trusted with anything of this nature and any powers granted to them would be abused, *ala* the FISA courts and spy agency surveillance of Americans. The changes in the law would have to be very specific to cover just pandemics. Fortunately, viral outbreaks are well-defined phenomena and not vague "terrorist threats".

There have been fewer than 100 deaths from coronavirus in the entire country so far. This "pandemic" is a non-event. Only in the elderly Italian populations, with incompetent socialized medicine hospitals, have people been dying at higher rates. Even then, the number is fewer than 2,000 deaths.

Every year, there are many different viral outbreaks that kill thousands of people. In 2022, you can bet your bottom dollar that the Democrats will do this again to try to take back the House that they will surely lose this year. The pattern of all of these fearmongering pandemics has coincided with election cycles. Enough is enough.

Never Again

August 16, 2020- by Steven E. Greer

This false Wuhan virus pandemic has set some extremely dangerous precedents that need to be reversed as soon as President Trump and the Republican Congress take over. If quick action is not taken, they will take root and become the accepted norm.

The fear of the invisible virus pandemic is powerful and has been exploited by the far-left. There's nothing to prevent it from being exploited by a far-right government next time.

The far-left Marxists have called our bluff. They exposed that the United States Constitution is just a piece of paper. No one was willing to defend it, not even Chief Justice Roberts.

The First Amendment has been rendered meaningless. The Supreme Court has ruled repeatedly this year that state leaders can do whatever they want regarding arbitrary lockdown orders, even if they clearly apply only to places of worship and not casinos or large riots in the streets.

The Supreme Court has also repeatedly ruled that states have the right to arbitrarily make fiat or decrees that drastically harm their citizens. The result has been mass culling of humans in the case of nursing homes and loss of livelihood in millions of others. School children and college kids have had their lives permanently altered by these arbitrary politically motivated decisions.

These policies put in place to "flatten the curve" with masks and social distancing have not a scintilla of science to support them. The CDC has completely dropped the ball here. It is the agency created specifically to "control diseases".

At the NIH, Anthony Fauci epitomizes the Deep State permanent bureaucrat, never elected to anything, who somehow was given immense powers to shut down global economies. The boss of Anthony Fauci, Francis Collins, also has been in power far too long. The NIH and the CDC are corrupted to the core.

ow can we fix the damage done and prevent it from ever happening again?

The first step would be to pass legislation against all of the above decrees. There should be federal acts that make it illegal to shut down businesses and mandate personal protective equipment because there is no scientific justification for it. In fact, the results of this global experiment are coming in now and countries with the least restrictive lockdowns had the fastest recovery to herd immunity without mass deaths that the fearmongers claimed would happen.

Then, there needs to be some sort of federal statue, or Supreme Court ruling, that allows the Department of Justice to take over cities that have run amok, such as Seattle, Portland, and New York. All of the governors and mayors have clearly broken their oaths of office for political means. It should be possible to oust a bad mayor like Bill DeBlasio in the same way that they recall leaders in California or Washington.

The first step toward putting that nation back on the right track will occur on November 3rd. There should be a purging of these spineless communist sympathizers turning a false pandemic into an opportunity for political power. Then, the weak Republican governors caving in to pressures to lockdown need to be ousted, starting with Ohio's Mike DeWine.

And finally, the DOJ needs to arrest the billionaire communists who orchestrated all of this scamdemic. That includes the CEO's of the globalist conglomerates who own the propaganda news media and social media. We need an Attorney General willing to prosecute treason and sedition.

In bullet-points, the plans of action are:

1) Reform the CDC. It is corrupted to the core and cannot handle pandemics. Reform the NIH as well. Never again should a 79-year-old unelected bureaucrat like Tony Fauci be given powers to close down a global economy.

2) Outlaw lockdown mandates and mask mandates. Zero science is behind them.

3) Get a Supreme Court willing to enforce the First Amendment. Lockdowns violate the constitution.

4) Make new laws to allow DOJ to more easily take over failing cities with rogue leaders breaking oaths of office.

5) Reform media coverage of pandemics: It is not protected by First Amendment to fearmonger. Perhaps coverage in the press would be first cleared by the CDC or some bipartisan congressional committee.

Steven E. Greer, MD: Curriculum Vitae

Education

- **M.D.**: The Ohio State University College of Medicine, Columbus, Ohio
- **B.A.**: The Ohio State University Fisher College of Business. Major: Finance:

Medical Work Experience

- **Quality of Life Clinic** Founder/CEO. Concierge medicine, wound care/limb salvage, and medical advocacy services
- **Research Project Director**- New York Veterans Affairs Medical Center/ The Institute of Reconstructive Plastic Surgery, New York University Medical Center. Responsible for the operations of a two-year $408,000 multicenter wound healing research project and management of a Ph.D. Research Nurse (see Grants section).
- **Postdoctoral Clinical Wound Healing Fellow**- The Developmental Biology and Repair Laboratory of Michael T. Longaker, The Institute of Reconstructive Plastic Surgery, New York University Medical Center
- **General Surgery/Plastic Surgery Residency**- New York University Medical Center
- **General Surgery-** Mount Sinai Hospital and Jackson Memorial Hospital, Miami

Academic Projects

- **The Bellevue Wound Healing and Research Center**: initiated the creation of a multidisciplinary wound healing and research center.
- **The New York University Wound Healing Center**: after the Bellevue wound center, was invited by the Chairman of Plastic Surgery to help develop the NYU wound healing center.

Financial Work Experience

- **The Healthcare Channel** (http://thehcc.tv/) Founder/CEO. Provides business information in multimedia format to institutional investors and healthcare executives via subscription.
- **Fox Business Network** and **Wall Street Journal** contributor. Contract partner with **Thomson Reuters** for healthcare content creation.
- **Merrill Lynch** Strategic Investment Group. Director. Global Healthcare Portfolio Manager for a $10B long/short internal hedge fund
- **The SG Healthcare Fund**. Founder
- **Sigma Capital** Management. Partner. A subsidiary fund of SAC Capital
- **Donaldson, Lufkin & Jenrette** Securities Corporation, then **Credit-Suisse First Boston** after the merger with DLJ. Research Analyst, Medical Device/Diagnostics/Biotech

Books and Mainstream Publications

1. Greer SE. "**Tony's Virus**" New York. Amazon and Barnes & Noble presses. 2020
2. Greer SE. "**The Medical Advocate**" New York. Amazon and Barnes & Noble presses. 2019-2020
3. Greer SE. "**Rules to Stop Radicals**" New York. Amazon and Barnes & Noble presses. 2019-2020
4. Greer SE (Editor-in-Chief), Benhaim P, Lorenz HP, Chang J, Hedrick MH (Eds.). "**The Handbook of Plastic Surgery**" New York: Marcel Dekker, 2004
5. Greer SE. "**Inside ObamaCare's Grant-Making**" Op-Ed in The Wall Street Journal. June 4, 2012
6. Greer SE. "**Pork is Clogging CMMI's Arteries**" Letter section in The Wall Street Journal. June 20, 2012

Legal Publications

1. Greer SE. *Greer v Mehiel*. 19-1262. The Supreme Court of the United States. Petition for writ of certiorari. April 20, 2020
2. Greer SE. *Greer v Mehiel*. 19-1262. The Supreme Court of the United States. Rule 44 motion. July 17, 2020

Federal Grants

1. B2108RC/VA Merit Review Grant, 10/01/99-10/01/2001 (Principal Investigator: Longaker)[151] awarded $408,280: **Investigation of Subatmospheric Pressure Dressing on Pressure Ulcer Healing.**
2. NCRR M01 RR00096, 6/21/99-6/20/2000 (Principal Investigator: Longaker) **Controlled Study of Subatmospheric Pressure Dressing on Below-Knee Amputation Wounds.** The NIH-funded General Clinical Research Center, physically located at Bellevue but a distinct entity, accepted the application for the study listed above to be conducted at their facility. (The VA also approved this grant, but did not provide funding given that they had funded the other study)
3. NCRR M01 RR00096, 6/21/99-6/20/2000 (Principal Investigator: Greer): **Application of Outcome Data to Pressure Ulcer Healing.** The NIH-funded General Clinical Research Center, physically located at Bellevue Hospital but a distinct entity, accepted the application for the study listed above to be conducted at their facility.
4. Private Industry Grant, KCI inc., 10/31/98-10/31/99 (Principal Investigator: Greer) $64,000, 1998: **A Controlled Study Comparing the Effectiveness of Subatmospheric Pressure Dressing to Normal Saline Wet-To-Moist Dressing on Pressure Ulcers**

[151] Steven Greer designed the trials, wrote the grant applications, and conducted all clinical care and data gathering. However, being a resident in training lacking "attending" status, Michael Longaker was listed as PI

Journal Articles

1. Greer SE, Matarasso A, Wallach S, Simon G, Longaker MT: **The Importance of the Nasal-to-Cervical Relationship to the Profile and Rhinoplasty Surgery.** *Plastic and Reconstructive Surgery*. 108(2):522-31; discussion 532-5. 2001
2. Greer SE, Grossi EA, Chin D, Longaker MT. **Subatmospheric Pressure Dressing for Closure of Saphenous Vein Donor-Site Wound Complications.** *Annals of Thoracic Surgery*, 71(3):1038-1040, 2001
3. Greer SE: **A Lesson from the High-Tech Economic Boom: Utilize the Competitive Advantage of Plastic Surgery.** *Plastic and Reconstructive Surgery*, 107(2):598-601, 2001
4. Puckett CL, Greer SE: **A Lesson from the High-Tech Economic Boom: Utilize the Competitive Advantage of Plastic Surgery.** Discussion. *Plastic and Reconstructive Surgery*, 107(2):602-603, 2001
5. Greer SE: **Whither Subatmospheric Pressure Dressing?** Editorial. *Ann Plast Surg*, 45(3):332-4, 2000
6. Greer SE, Matarasso A, Wallach S, Simon G, Longaker MT: **The Nasal-to-Cervical Relationship of Rhinoplasty Surgery.** *Plastic Surgical Forum*, 2000
7. Greer SE, Longaker MT, Cutting C, McCarthy JG, Shaw W, Lorenz HP: **The Gold Standard for Acceptable Resolution of Projected Digital Photographic Images in Plastic Surgery.** *Plastic Surgical Forum,* 2000
8. Greer SE, MD, Adelman M, MD, Kasabian A, MD, Galiano R, MD, Scott R, MD, Longaker MT, MD: **The Use of Subatmospheric Pressure Dressing to Close Lymphocutaneous Fistulas of the Groin**. *Brit J Plast Surg*, 53(6):484-487, 2000
9. Matarasso A, Greer SE, Longaker MT: **The True Hanging Columella: Simplified Diagnosis and**

Treatment Using a Modified Direct Approach. *Plastic and Reconstructive Surgery*, 106(2):469-474, 2000

10. Matarasso A, Greer SE, Longaker MT: **The True Hanging Columella: Simplified Diagnosis and Treatment Using a Modified Direct Approach.** *Plastic Surgical Forum*, 2000
11. Greer SE, Longaker MT, Margiotta M: **Preliminary Results from a Multicenter, Randomized, Controlled, Study of the Use of Subatmospheric Pressure Dressing for Pressure Ulcer Healing.** *Wound Repair and Regeneration*. 7(4); 255, 1999
12. Greer SE, Longaker MT, Margiotta M, Mathews AJ, Kasabian A: **The Use of Subatmospheric Pressure Dressing for the Coverage of Radial Forearm Free Flap Donor-Site Exposed Tendon Complications.** *Ann Plast Surg*. 43(5):551-554, November 1999
13. Greer SE, Duthie E, Cartolano B, Koehler KM, Maydick-Youngberg D, Longaker MT: **Techniques for Applying Subatmospheric Pressure Dressing to Wounds in Difficult Regions of Anatomy.** *Journal of Wound Ostomy Continence Nursing*. 26(5); 250-3, September 1999
14. Greer SE, Kasabian A, Thorne C, Borud L, Sims CD, Hsu M: **The Use of a Subatmospheric Pressure Dressing to Salvage a Gustilo Grade IIIB Open Tibia Fracture with Concomitant Osteomyelitis and Avert a Free Flap.** Letter. *Annals of Plastic Surgery*, 41(6); 687, Dec 1998

Presentations and Television Appearances

1. Greer SE, Regular guest on **The Fox Business Network**, 2008 to 2013
2. Greer SE, Guest on **CNBC's Larry Kudlow Show**, 2013
3. Greer SE, Guest on **MSNBC's Dylan Ratigan Show**, 2012
4. Greer SE, FDA **Rejection of Cyberonics Depression Device**. Kudlow and Cramer Show. CNBC. August 12, 2004
5. Greer SE, Guest on **CNBC's Kudlow and Cramer Show**. CNBC. April 27, 2004
6. Matarasso, A, Greer SE, Wallach S, Longaker MT, Simon, G. **The Importance of the Nasal-to-Cervical Relationship in Rhinoplasty Surgery**. American Association of Plastic Surgeons-80th Annual Meeting. Charleston, SC. May 16, 2001.
7. Greer SE, Longaker MT, Cutting C, McCarthy JG, Shaw W, Lorenz HP: **The Gold Standard for Acceptable Resolution of Projected Digital Photographic Images in Plastic Surgery.** American Society of Plastic Surgeons- 69th annual meeting, Los Angeles, California, October 15, 2000
8. Matarasso A, Greer SE, Longaker MT: **The True Hanging Columella: Simplified Diagnosis and Treatment Using a Modified Direct Approach.** American Society of Plastic Surgeons- 69th annual meeting, Los Angeles, California, October 15, 2000
9. Greer SE, Matarasso A, Wallach S, Simon G, Longaker MT: **The Nasal-to-Cervical Relationship of Rhinoplasty Surgery.** Accepted for poster presentation at the 69th annual ASPS meeting, Los Angeles, California, October 15, 2000
10. Matarasso A, Greer SE, Longaker MT: **The True Hanging Columella: Simplified Diagnosis and**

Treatment Using a Modified Direct Approach. Presented at the fifth annual Rhinoplasty Society meeting, Orlando, Florida, May 11, 2000

11. Greer SE, Matarasso A, Wallach S, Simon G, Longaker MT: **The Nasal-to-Cervical Relationship of Rhinoplasty Surgery.** Presented at the fifth annual Rhinoplasty Society meeting, Orlando, Florida, May 2000
12. Greer SE, Houston V: **A Proposal to Treat Land Mine Amputation Wounds Using Subatmospheric Pressure Dressing.** Presented at the World Health Organization, 2 United Nations Plaza, New York, NY to the Executive Director of the WHO, Dr. Bassani, November 18, 1999
13. Greer SE, Longaker MT, Margiotta M, Mathews AJ, Kasabian A: **The Use of Subatmospheric Pressure Dressing for the Coverage of Radial Forearm Free Flap Donor-Site Exposed Tendon Complications.** Presented at the International Society of Reconstructive Microsurgeons, UCLA Medical Center, Los Angeles, CA June 22, 1999
14. Greer SE: **Subatmospheric Pressure Dressing: Clinical Applications and Research Opportunities.** Presented at the Grand Rounds for the Division of Plastic Surgery, Yale University, New Haven, CT, April 15, 1999
15. Greer SE, Longaker MT, Margiotta M: **Preliminary Results from a Multicenter, Randomized, Controlled, Study of the Use of Subatmospheric Pressure Dressing for Pressure Ulcer Healing.** Accepted for presentation at the Joint Meeting of the European Tissue Repair Society and The Wound Healing Society. Bordeaux, France August, 1999
16. Greer SE: **Subatmospheric Pressure Dressing: Orthopedic Clinical Applications and Research**

Opportunities. Jacoby Hospital Orthopedic Conference. New York, NY January, 1999

17. Clarkson MW, Greer SE, Sullivan MJ, Danahey D, Siegle RJ,: **The Effects Of Estrogen on Photoaged Skin and Chemical Peeling**. Presented at the 1994 William H. Saunders Lectureship, Columbus, Ohio.
18. Greer SE, Townsend M: **Motorcycle Helmet Use and Mechanisms of Injury**. Landacre Research Conference. Columbus, Ohio, 1993

Testimonials

April 2, 2020- "Wow. Dr. Greer, this is the most vital 20-minutes we've done on the radio, and we're just so privileged to have you."

April 9, 2020- "This is the man who told us about hydroxychloroquine and the Z-Pak weeks ago. Weeks ago, he said..."

May 4, 2020, "Well, you are the man. You are the man. You are so ahead of the curve. I got to tell you right now—and-and I'm telling you—everything that you talked about, Dr. Greer—and I keep giving you a shoutout on the program, and I did-as I did today—you talked about—and we played the audio, uh last week, played the audio—of you just saying very casually, "oh, we have-we have some drugs for this virus." And you said Rem-Remdisivir. You said-you talked about hydroxychloroquine and Z-PAK. You were there…"

May 12, 2020- "You were the first to talk about remdesivir… You know, Dr. Greer we appreciate your expertise. We appreciate you being with us. Come back soon. Yeah, let's talk soon, uh, because everything you've said comes to fruition."

Joe Piscopo
The Joe Piscopo Show
AM970 radio

Index

Y

Made in the USA
Las Vegas, NV
03 April 2021

20724624R10111